Spotlight SCIENCE

7

Keith JOHNSON ★ Sue ADAMSON ★ Gareth WILLIAMS

With the active support of: Lawrie Ryan, Bob Wakefield, Anne Goldsworthy,
Roger Frost, Helen Davis, Valerie Wood-Robinson, Phil Bunyan,
Adrian Wheaton, John Bailey, Janet Hawkins,
Ann Johnson, Graham Adamson, Diana Williams.

SPIRAL EDITION

™ Nelson Thornes
a Wolters Kluwer business

First published in 1993
Second edition published in 2000 by:
Nelson Thornes (Publishers) Ltd

Nelson Thornes Ltd
Delta Place
27 Bath Road
CHELTENHAM
GL53 7TH
United Kingdom

08 / 10

A catalogue record for this book is available from the British Library

ISBN 13: 978-0-7487-8455-4

Illustrations and typesetting by Tech-Set, Gateshead, Tyne & Wear.

Printed and Bound in China by Midas Printing International Ltd.

Acknowledgements

The authors and publishers are grateful to the following for permission to reproduce photographs:

Allsport: 11T (Paul Severn), 153 (David Cannon); Ancient Art and Architecture Collection: 11B; Ardea: 28TL; Biophoto Associates: 48CR, 51CL, 55; Bridgeman Art Library: 61 (Petworth House, West Sussex, UK), 131 (Musee d'Orsay, Paris, France/Bulloz); Bruce Coleman: 48BC (MPL Fogden), 50TR (Gerald Cubitt), BL (Alain Compost), 51CR (Hans Reinhard), 52CL (Jules Cowan), B (Dr Eckart Pott), 73 (Erich Crichton), 124T (Hans Reinhard), BL (John R Anthony), BC (John Markham), 133BL (Jane Burton), 137TL (Jane Burton), B (Neil McAllister), 141B (Mark Taylor), 142BL (Ron Lilley), 145B (John Cancalosi), 147 (Jane Burton), 155R (Frank Greenaway), 157 (Rod Williams), 158L (Patrick Clement), R (Jane Burton); CEFIC: 75; Chris Fairclough Colour Library: 134; Collections: 88T (Anthea Sieveking), 91TR, CR, B (Anthea Sieveking), 94 (Anthea Sieveking); Cotswold Wildlife Park: 50TL, CL, CR; DUPONT: 24TR; Ecoscene: 77L (Platt); Frank Lane Picture Agency: 53T (W Howes), 58T (W Wisniewski), 138BR (M Newman), 140BL (MJ Thomas), 142C (AR Hamblin), 142BR (M Walker), 149 (Tom and Pam Gardener), 154 (H Buiz), 155L; Geoscience Features Photolibrary: 137TR (Dr B Booth), 137CL, CR; Heather Angel Biofotos: 48TC, TR, 52CR; Heinz: 110; ICI: 31B, 115; Image Bank: 102 (JW Banagan), cover; Israeli Tourist Office: 64; J Allen Cash Photolibrary: 27, 46, 140BR, 156B; John Walmsley Photolibrary: 40, 84TR, BL, BC, 91CL, 95 inset; Keith Johnson: 13, 151; London Fire Brigade: 105; Martyn Chillmaid: 4, 6, 7, 14T, 16, 22, 24L, CR, BR, 25T, 26C, 28B, 38, 56, 74, 76, 79, 80, 81, 82, 93, 110, 112, 114, 118, 121, 130B, 132B, 133T; Moorfields Eye Hospital: 98TR; Muscular Dystrophy Group: 106B; NASA: 33R; Natural History Photographic Agency: 124BR (Agence Nature), 132T (Stephen Dalton); Oxford Scientific Films: 48TL (Rodger Jackson), CL (David Thompson), CC (London Scientific Films), BL (GI Bernard), BCL (Alistair Shay), BCR (DG Fox), BR (GI Bernard), 51TL (Mike Birkhead), CC (Michael Fogden), BL (Ben Osborne), BR (Stan Osolinski), 52T (Tim Shepherd), 53B (Mark Pidgeon), 127B (Mark Ulrich); Panasonic: 12; Planet Earth Pictures: 128; Professional Sport: 33L; Rex Features: 34 (Today); Robert Harding Picture Library: 84BR, 95 main (Michael J Howell), 109, 116TR (Gary Bighorn, Int'l Stock); Science Photolibrary: 24B, 54T (Bruce Iverson) B (Andrew Syred), 58B (Chuck Brown), 62T (David Scharf), 77R (Will McIntyre), 86L (Petit Format/Nestle), 88CL, CR, B (Petit Format/Nestle), 87 (Don Fawcett), 90 (Katrina Thomas), 98BR (Alex Bartel), 130T (Sidney Moulds), C (Claude Nuridsany and Marie Perennou), 133BR (Alfred Pasiela), 135 (Soames Summerhays), 138L (Adam Hart), TR (George Bernard), 140T (Michael Marten), 141TL (Martin Bond), 145T (Sinclair Stammers), 148 (Oscar Burriel, Latin Stock), 156T (Hattie Young); SeaLife Centre (Holdings): 50BR; Silvercross Ltd: 72B; Stockmarket: 31CT, 72T (ZEFA), 116BR (ZEFA), 126 (ZEFA-Kalt); Stone: Cover (Tony Duffy), 14B (Jon Gray), 23 (Tony Duffy), 36 (Jean François Causse), 44T (Peter Correz), B (Chad Slattery), 59 (John PA Carter), 65TL, TR (Jean-Marc Truchet), 83 (Ron Sutherland), 84TL (Andrew Cox), 85 (Lisa Valder), 91TL (Lisa Valder), 127T (Jane Burton); Timothy Woodcock Photolibrary: 62B; Wilderness Photographic: 43 (John Noble).

Contents

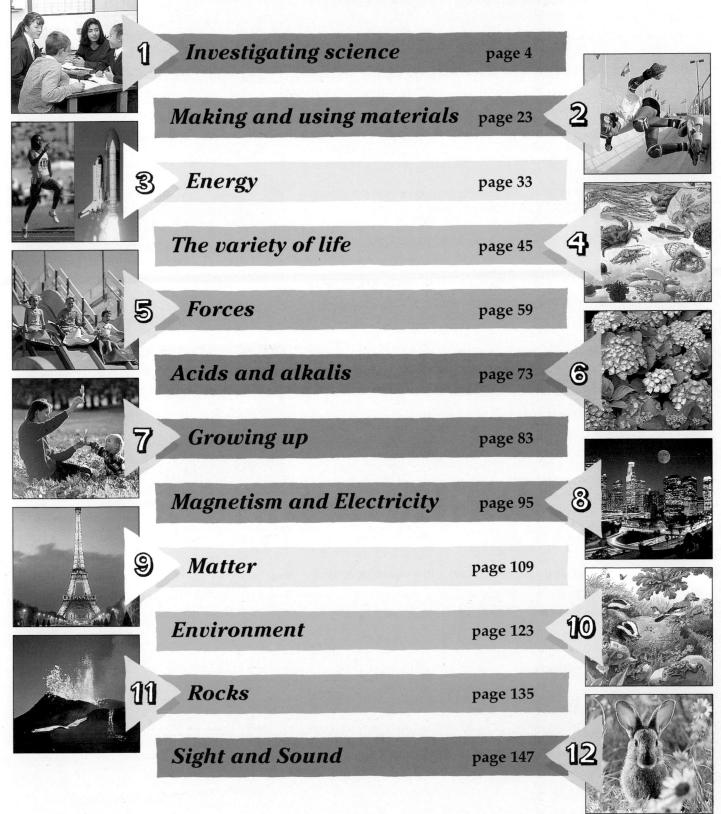

How do detectives **investigate** a murder? They look for clues and then see what the clues mean.

We do this in science. We investigate by asking questions and looking for clues. We collect evidence and then we try to work out what the evidence means. We look for patterns in the evidence.

To investigate you need to use some basic skills. This part of the book helps you with these skills. One of these skills is **observing**.

Observing

▶ Are you a good observer? Try closing your eyes and counting how many things you can remember about this room.

▶ Now look carefully round the room. How many unusual things can you see?

Are there any notices on the walls? What do they say?

Is there any fire-fighting equipment? Why is it in that position?

▶ Your teacher will give you some **safety glasses**. Look at them carefully. How are they designed to protect your eyes?

Are they clean? If not, what should you do?

Keep them on until you are used to them. Remember your eyes can be easily damaged. Just think how your life would change if you were blind!

Look at the safety triangle sign. This sign is used to warn you of a possible danger! Whenever you see it, make sure you know what you must do to work safely.

How many hidden objects can you find?

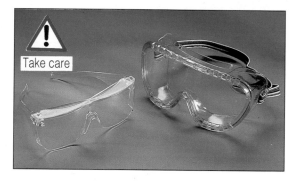

Your teacher will give your group a test-tube and a small piece of a chemical.

Put some water in the test-tube (about three-quarters full).

When your group is ready, drop the chemical into the water and observe it carefully. Write down or draw everything that happens. These are your **observations**.

When the experiment has finished, discuss your observations with each other.
Do you agree on everything that you saw? If not, what should you do now?

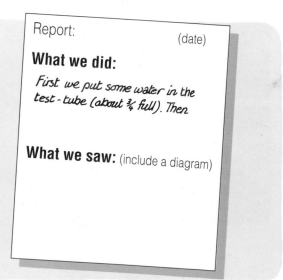

Report: (date)

What we did:
First we put some water in the test-tube (about ¾ full). Then

What we saw: (include a diagram)

► Look at the cartoon below, and discuss it in your group.
How many **un**safe things can you observe? Ten?

For each one, write down why it is unsafe and what **should** be done to make it safe.

Unsafe thing	Why is it unsafe?	What should be done?

Things to do

1 Each science lab usually has a set of rules (a sort of Highway Code). Find the rules for your lab.
Read them and then write down the **reason** for having each rule.

2 Draw a safety poster for your science lab. Concentrate on one of the rules, and think how to get your message across clearly.

3 Look around your home, searching for unsafe situations where accidents might happen. Draw up a list.
Talk to your family about anything that should be made safer.

4 Draw a safety poster for your home.

5 Imagine you have a pen-pal in your last school. Write a letter telling her or him how you feel about today's science lesson.

Observing

Observing is an important skill in science.
It helps you to be *scientific*.

▶ Are you observant? Write down (if you can):
  • the colour of the paint in your bedroom
  • the colour of the school gates
  • the shape of the school gates
  • the number or name on the door of this room.

▶ Look at the photographs. Can you identify them?
  Write down the name of each object.

Good observers use *all* their senses, not just their eyes.

▶ Close your eyes and *listen* – how many different sounds can
  you identify?

  Imagine eating a packet of crisps with your eyes shut.
  What observations could you make? Make a list.

Place a candle so that everyone in your group can observe it.
Before you light it, think about *safety*: what needs to be done?

Then light the wick and observe the flame.

Write down as many observations as you can (about the flame,
the candle and the wick).

Draw a labelled diagram of the candle and flame.
On your diagram, label something which is **solid**.
Then label something which is **liquid**.
Then label something which is not solid or liquid, but is a **gas**.

What can you observe when you blow out the candle?
Can you describe the smell?

The Bunsen burner

▶ Look at a Bunsen burner carefully.
  How many parts has it got?

  Where does the gas come in?

  How can you change the size of the
  air-hole?

▶ Follow these instructions to light a
  Bunsen burner:

1. Put your Bunsen burner on a heat-proof mat.
2. Push the rubber tube firmly on to the gas-tap.
3. Close the air-hole.
4. Put on your safety glasses and keep them on.
5. Get a 'light', turn the gas-tap and light the burner.
6. Open the air-hole slowly and observe the changes in
   the flame.

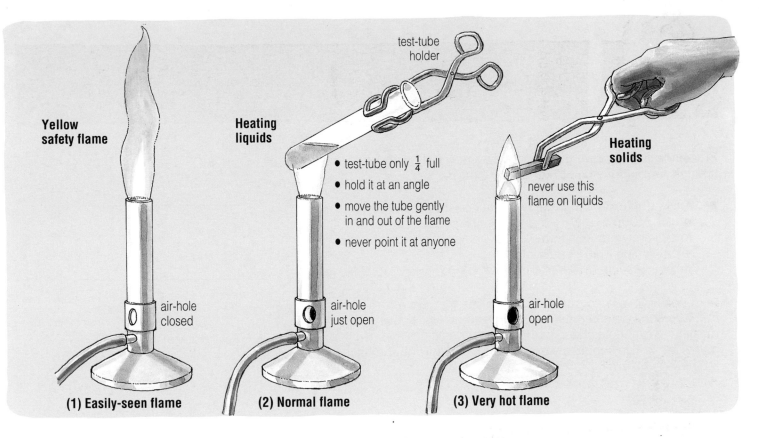

Yellow safety flame

(1) Easily-seen flame

air-hole closed

Heating liquids

test-tube holder

- test-tube only $\frac{1}{4}$ full
- hold it at an angle
- move the tube gently in and out of the flame
- never point it at anyone

air-hole just open

(2) Normal flame

Heating solids

never use this flame on liquids

air-hole open

(3) Very hot flame

a Which flame should you use when you are not heating anything?

b Why is this called the safety flame?

c Which flame will you use most often for heating?

d Why should you always wear safety glasses when using a Bunsen burner?

Get a short piece of magnesium ribbon from your teacher. Hold it at arm's length in some tongs. Then move it into the flame (do not look directly at it). What happens? What is left?

Where is magnesium used:
- on November 5th?
- near a sinking ship?

Do you think a candle flame is as hot as a Bunsen flame? How could you use two pieces of magnesium ribbon to test this?

Magnesium in action

1 Draw a diagram of a Bunsen burner and label it.
Where do you think the flame is hottest?

2 Explain:
a) how to light a Bunsen burner
b) how to get a normal heating flame
c) how to get an easily-seen flame
d) how to get a smaller flame
e) how to get a very hot flame.

3 A chip-pan fire in your kitchen is very dangerous. If it ever happens, why should you **not** throw water on it?
Why should you get hold of a wet towel and what should be done with it?

4 Write a short poem about flames.

5 Who was Robert Wilhelm Bunsen? Where did he live, and when? (He lost an eye because he didn't use safety glasses!)

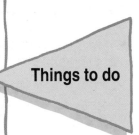

Things to do

Measuring

In science, just observing with your eyes may not be accurate enough. You often need to **measure** things.

▶ For example, look at these two black lines: which *looks* longer, A or B?
To be sure, you need to measure each line accurately, with a ruler. Which is longer, A or B?
What is the length of each, in mm?

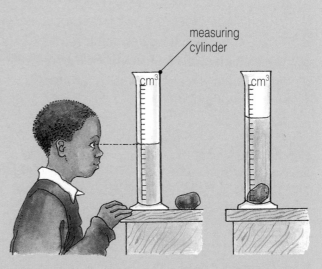

An optical illusion
Which line is the longer?

In this lesson you are going to use thermometers, clocks and measuring cylinders. Each of these instruments has a *scale* with marks on it. You should always measure carefully on the scale, to the *nearest mark*.

Using a measuring cylinder

This measures in units called **centimetres-cubed**, written **cm³**.

Look at the scale on a measuring cylinder or jug. What is the maximum (biggest) **volume** it can measure?

Count the number of divisions between two of the numbers on the scale. How big is *one* division (in cm³)?

Pour in some water, until it is about half-full.
Then take the reading, making sure that:
• the measuring cylinder is *vertical*, not sloping
• your eye is *level* with the bottom of the water surface.
What is the volume of the water?

Practise reading the scale with different amounts of water.
Check your partner's readings.

If you have time …

Finding the volume of a pebble

Now gently drop in a pebble (or another object that sinks in water).
Why does the water level rise?

What is the volume reading now? (This is the volume of the water *and* the pebble.)

How can you work out the volume of the pebble? What is the volume of the pebble, in cm³?

Try again with a different amount of water. Do you get the same result? Try it a third time.

What is the advantage of *repeating* results like this?

	Volume of water (cm³)	Volume of water + pebble (cm³)	∴ Volume of pebble (cm³)
1			
2			
3			
		Average =	

Using a thermometer

This measures in units called **degrees Celsius**, written **°C**.

Look at the scale on the thermometer. What is the maximum (highest) **temperature** it can measure? What is the minimum?

Look at the smallest divisions on the scale. How big is one of these divisions (in °C)?

What is the temperature of the thermometer now?
What happens if you warm the bulb end gently with your hand?
Can you explain this?

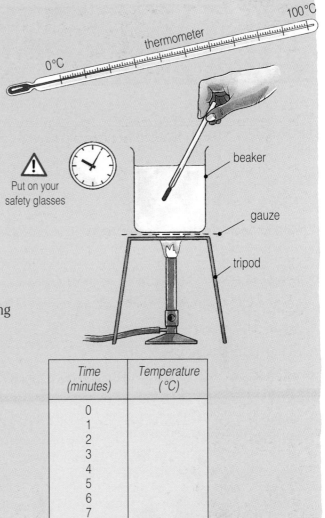

Put on your safety glasses

beaker

gauze

tripod

Now use a measuring cylinder (see the opposite page) to measure 100 cm³ of water into a beaker.
Copy out the table ready for your results.
Take the temperature of the water. Record it on the first line of your table.

Put the beaker on a tripod. Light a Bunsen burner and start heating the water. Stir the water gently and take its temperature every minute, for 8 minutes.

Look at the results in your table. Is there a pattern? (!Lcave the beaker and tripod to cool before moving them!)

How would your results be different if you used:
- more water?
- a smaller flame?

If you have time, plot a line graph of your results, with **time** along the bottom and **temperature** up the side.

Time (minutes)	Temperature (°C)
0	
1	
2	
3	
4	
5	
6	
7	
8	

Things to do

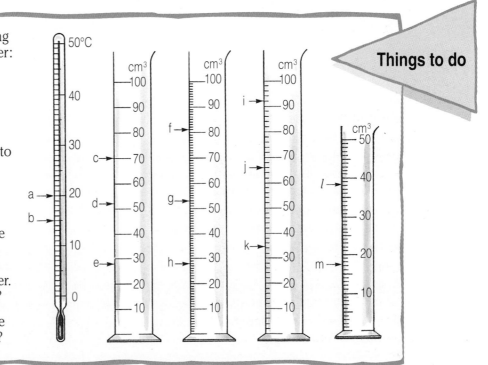

1 Study the diagrams. What is the reading at each of the arrows (a to m)? (Remember: you always read to the nearest mark.)

2 Make a list of 5 measuring instruments used in your home.

3 If you have a measuring jug and a marker pen, how could you use bath-time to find the volume of your body?

4 A pack of 500 sheets of paper is 50 mm thick. How thick is one sheet?

5 A problem: you need to find the volume of a stone but it is too large to fit into your measuring cylinder. It will fit into a beaker, and you have enough water to fill the beaker. How can you find the volume of the stone?

6 Which of these cylinders would you use to find the volume of a small button? Why?

More measuring

Here are three investigations for you to do – in any order.
Plan your time carefully in order to finish them all.

Using a top-pan balance

A top-pan balance measures the **mass** of an object, in grams (**g**) or in kilograms (**kg**).
(People using this balance sometimes say they are 'weighing' an object, because weight and mass are connected.)

Make sure that the balance shows **zero** before you start.

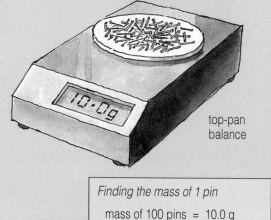

top-pan balance

- What is the mass of this book**?**

- What is the mass of a 10p coin**?**

- Estimate the mass of a 20p coin, and then measure it.

- What is the mass of one paper-clip**?**
  If you have 20 identical paper-clips, how can you find the mass of one paper-clip more accurately**?**

- How can you find the mass of 100 cm³ of water**?**

Finding the mass of 1 pin

mass of 100 pins = 10.0 g

$$\frac{\text{average}}{\text{mass of 1 pin}} = \frac{10.0}{100} = 0.1 \text{ g}$$

Investigating a pendulum

Finding the time for 1 swing

time for 10 swings = 12 s

$$\therefore \text{ time for 1 swing} = \frac{12}{10} = 1.2 \text{ s}$$

You can make a pendulum from a piece of string with a weight or 'bob' at the end of it.

Use a stop-clock to time the swings. One swing is one complete 'round-trip' – from one side, through the middle to the other side and back again.

Timing one swing is not very accurate – it is much better to time 10 complete swings, and then divide the time by 10.

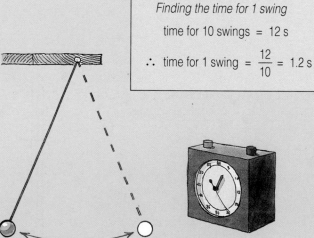

stop clock

- Investigate how the time for a swing depends on the **length** of the pendulum. What happens if you halve or double the length of the string**?**

  How many times should you take each measurement**?**
  Why should you repeat the measurements**?**

If you have time ...

- Investigate how the time for a swing depends on the **mass** of the bob (you can add plasticine round the bob). Make sure that you keep the length of the string the same so that it is a **fair test**.

Length (cm)	Time for 10 swings (seconds)	Time for 1 swing (seconds)

Measuring your body

Everyone's body is different – and we each have different measurements.

Make these measurements and keep a record of them:

- your height (in cm)
- the length from your elbow to the tip of your middle finger (in cm). This length used to be called your 'cubit'.
- your mass (in kg)
- the temperature of your armpit (in °C)
- your normal breathing rate (breaths per minute)
- your normal pulse rate (beats per minute or 'bpm')

A **pulse monitor** can be used to measure your pulse rate. Attach the sensor to your body, and connect it to a computer:

Record your normal pulse for 2 minutes.
What is the average?

Run on the spot for 1 minute.
Then record your pulse rate… until it returns to normal.

How long does it take for your pulse rate to return to normal?
This is a measure of your fitness.

Plot a graph of your **pulse rate** against **time**.
In your group, compare the graphs. Can you see a pattern?

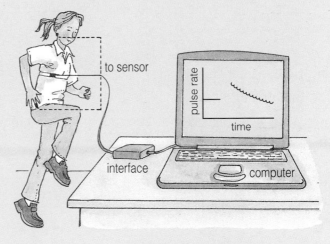

Measuring your pulse rate

Things to do

1 Take your pulse several times each day for the next 3 days. Does it vary? When is it highest? When is it lowest?

2 Why is it more accurate to time 10 swings of a pendulum rather than just one swing?

3 Noah built his Ark boat to be 300 cubits long. How long is your cubit? How long would the Ark have been if you had built it? Why is a cubit not used today?

4 An empty beaker 'weighs' 50 grams. When it contains 100 cm³ of water, it 'weighs' 150 g. What is the mass of 100 cm³ of water?

5 50 nails have a mass of 200 grams. What is the average mass of one nail? Why have we used the word 'average' here?

6 A measuring cylinder contains 20 cm³ of water. When 4 marbles are put in the water, the reading becomes 32 cm³.
What is the average volume of a marble?

7 An Italian boy called Galileo was the first person to notice that a pendulum swings with a constant time for each swing.

Research, using an encyclopedia (a book or a ROM) or the Internet, to find out:
a) When did Galileo live?
b) What else is he famous for?

Galileo as an old man

Interpreting and concluding

We have looked at the skills of observing and measuring. In this lesson we are looking at another skill: **interpreting**. Interpreting means making sense of information or *data*.

In science you need to interpret information that is shown in different ways. It may be in tables or on graphs. Or it may be in symbols.

▶ Look at the symbols shown here:
For each one, write down what the symbol means.

1 ⚠	2 (30)	3 🧺 40°	4
In this book	A road sign	On clothes	On a camera
5 ✂	6 ✖	7 ☠	8 ▶
On paper	On a bottle	On a bottle	In this book

▶ Here is a bar-chart of shoe sizes for a class of teenagers.

Interpret this chart to answer these questions:

a What is the biggest shoe size shown on the graph?

b What is the most common shoe size?

c What is the least common shoe size?

d How many people have size 4 shoes?

e How many people are there in this class?

Look around the room and count the number of people you think have 'light' hair, 'dark' hair or 'red' hair.

Draw a bar-chart of your information. Label your chart.

Other people's charts may be different. Why is this?

▶ The table below shows some data on stereo radio recorders.

Interpret this information to answer these questions:

f Which is the cheapest?

g Which is the one that has a tone control?

h Which one does not have a built-in microphone?

i Which one would you buy if you had £80 to spend?
Explain your reasons.

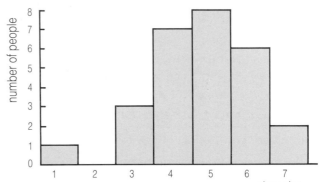

Key:
B = Built-in microphone   A = Autostop of tape
H = Headphone socket   R = autoReverse to
T = Tone control   play second side

Make	From	Price (£)	Size (cm)	Weight (kg)	General features	Cassette features	No. of decks	Cassette battery running costs
Realistic SCR90	Hong Kong	40	13 × 35 × 8	1.5	B	A	1	6p per hour
Sony CFS903L	Taiwan	80	20 × 44 × 13	2.6	B H T	A R	1	12p per hour
JVC RC-W210	Malaysia	80	16 × 62 × 17	4.9	H	A	2	10p per hour
Philips AW7392	Austria	70	15 × 50 × 14	3.0	B H	A R	2	6p per hour

► Chris put a Bunsen burner under a beaker of water for a few minutes, and then took it away.

She plotted a line-graph of temperature against time, as shown here:

She has drawn a 'line of best fit' through the crosses.

Look at the graph, and interpret it and '***draw conclusions***' to answer these questions:

j How can you tell that the water got hotter**?**

k What was the temperature of the water at the start**?**

l What was the temperature after 2 minutes**?**

m How long did it take to reach 60 °C**?**

n What was the highest temperature**?**

o What was the rise in temperature of the water**?**

p Which result do you think is wrong**?**

q What do you think this result should be**?** Why**?**

r For how many minutes do you think the Bunsen burner was under the beaker before she took it away**?**

s Imagine Chris had put more water in the beaker. Sketch the graph that you would expect. Explain why.

t Why is a line-graph better than a bar-chart here**?**

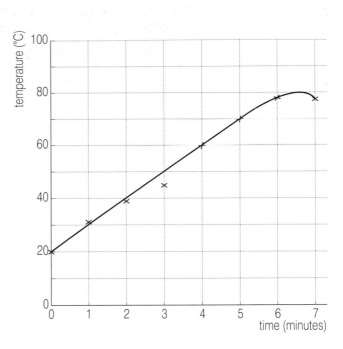

► Here is a photo of a sundial.

Your task is to ***interpret*** this photo by drawing up two lists:

Things that I can see on the photo. These are my **observations**.	Things that I can work out or **conclude** from the photo. These are my **conclusions**.
I can see a shadow. I can see a...	It is day-time. The sun is shining. I can tell that...

A sundial

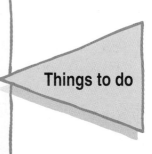

Things to do

1 In a survey of 30 pupils, 15 said that smoking should be banned, 10 said it shouldn't, and the rest didn't know.
From these data:
a) plot a bar-chart
b) plot a pie-chart.
Which chart do you prefer? Why?

2 Alan's answer to question **r** above was "The Bunsen burner was under the beaker for exactly 6 minutes". Emma disagreed. She said, "You can't be sure it was exactly 6 minutes". Who do you think was right? Justify and explain your answer.

3 Use the data below to plot a line-graph of temperature against time, like the one shown at the top of this page.

Time (minutes)	0	1	2	3	4	5
Temperature (°C)	10	30	45	55	60	62

Use your graph to find the temperature after $3\frac{1}{2}$ minutes.

4 Jessica heated some water with a Bunsen. Use a graph to decide which of her results may be wrong. What do you think they should be?

Time (minutes)	0	1	2	3	4	5	6
Temperature (°C)	15	26	41	48	59	67	81

Predicting and Evaluating

In science we are always trying to find ideas to explain our world. Then we use these ideas to make predictions.

For example, Lee was looking at some water that had spilled on the bench. The water was spreading across the bench. He said,

"I think water **always** flows downwards."

His idea was a **hypothesis** (*hi-poth-e-sis*).
He was **hypothesizing** (*hi-poth-e-size-ing*).

Anju had a better hypothesis. She said,

"I think water *always* flows downhill **because** gravity pulls it down."

These ideas are **hypotheses** (*hi-poth-e-sees*).
A hypothesis is a general idea about things which always happen.

A **prediction** is what you think will happen in a particular case.

From these hypotheses Pat made a **prediction**: "If you go to Egypt, you'll find the River Nile is flowing downhill."

The River Nile

▶ In your group, discuss these 3 boxes. Write down a hypothesis for each one. Start your sentence with 'I think' and include the word '**always**'. Then also try to include the word '**because**'.

| **1** | When you were observing a candle flame and a Bunsen flame, you saw that they both point ⌒ upwards. |

| **2** | Milk lasts longer if you put it in a fridge. |

| **3** | If you leave an ice-cube on the bench, it turns to water. Why is this? |

Hypotheses have to be tested, to see if they are true. We can do this by:
- making a prediction,
- collecting evidence, and then
- seeing if the evidence supports the prediction.

▶ Look at this cartoon. Sarah is testing a hypothesis:

Hypothesizing	**Predicting**	**Looking at the evidence**
A torch will always work well when it has new batteries.	*My torch is not working. It will work if I put in new batteries.*	*Drat! It is still not working. My hypothesis must be wrong.*

Evaluating the evidence

Jack and Sophie made a prediction:

"We think that the roaring flame of a Bunsen burner will be hotter than its normal flame." (see page 7)

Then they looked for evidence, like this:

Then they did the same again, two more times. Their results are shown here:

This was their conclusion:

"The roaring flame is hotter because the temperature went higher when we used the roaring flame."

Look at the details of their work carefully, and then answer these questions to **evaluate** it.

	Temperature with the normal flame (°C)	Temperature with the roaring flame (°C)
1	27	28
2	22	28
3	29	29

a Look at their conclusion. Do you think they have enough evidence to support their conclusion? Explain your answer.

b Look at their table. One of their results looks wrong ('anomalous'). Which one? Can you explain what might have happened?

c Safety is important. Do you think that Jack and Sophie were working safely? Explain your answer.

d Look at the way they did the investigation.
Find as many mistakes as you can, and list them. (Five?)
Then explain in detail how they could improve their investigation.

---

1 People usually hang out their washing to dry on a warm dry day.

Write down your **hypothesis** about this, using the word '**always**'.
Now make your sentence longer, using the word '**because**'.
Then write down a **prediction** you can make from your hypothesis.
How could you test your hypothesis?

2 Tom says, "*I think warm water always evaporates faster than cold water.*"
Use this hypothesis to write a prediction.
Then explain carefully how you could collect evidence to test your prediction.

3 Chloe says, "*I think metal objects can always be picked up by magnets.*"
Do you think she is right?
Use her hypothesis to write a prediction.
Then explain how you could collect enough evidence to test this prediction.

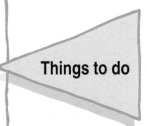

Things to do

Planning a fair test

In science you often have to **plan** an investigation.

When you plan something, you need to think ahead – to think of all the things you have to do.

An important part of your plan is to decide what you are going to change or **vary**.
The things that you change or vary are called **variables**.

Variables

These are all the things that can change or vary during your investigation. They are sometimes called **factors**.

In your plan you will:

- *decide which things should change.*
  These are the variables that you will measure, and then put the results in a table.

- *decide which things must not change.*
  These are the things you must keep the same, to make it a *fair test*.

Here is an example to explain this.

Variables are things that vary and change.

Suppose you had to carry out an investigation with the title:
'How does the amount of water given to a plant affect its growth?'

You could do this investigation by planting seeds in several pots. Then you could give each plant a different amount of water each day. You would measure the height of the plant each day.

The amount of water that you give to each plant is one of the variables. You could measure this variable with a measuring jug. This variable is sometimes called the **input** variable.

The height of the plant is another variable. You would measure this variable with a ruler. This is sometimes called the **outcome** variable.

It is important that the investigation is a **fair test**.

To make it a fair test, you have to **control** any other factors.
To control the other factors you would:

- use the **same** seeds in all the pots
- use the **same** soil in all the pots
- use the **same** size pots
- put the pots in the **same** position in the room.

These are called **control** variables.

You decide how much water to give the plants.
The amount of water is a variable.

input

You measure the height of the plant.
The height is a variable.

outcome

To make it a fair test, you must 'control' every other variable, to keep them the same.

In the boxes below are three investigations for you to plan.

Investigation 1

How does the **height** that a ball bounces depend upon the **surface** that it bounces on?

Plan:

What are you going to change?

What are you going to measure?

What are you going to keep the same (to make it a fair test)?

What can you do to make your results more reliable? Make a table for your results.

What kind of graph could you use to show your results?

Investigation 2

How does the **length** of an elastic band depend upon the **weights** hanging from it?

Plan:

What are you going to change?

What are you going to measure?

What are you going to keep the same (to make it a fair test)?

Make a table for your results.

What kind of graph could you use to show your results? Sketch what you think it will look like.

Investigation 3

How does your **pulse rate** depend upon the **amount of exercise** you do?

Plan:

What are you going to change?

What are you going to measure?

What are you going to control (to make it a fair test)?

Make a table for your results.

What kind of graph could you use to show your results?
Sketch what you think it will look like.

▶ If you have time, do one of these investigations.

1 Look again at Investigation 1 above.
a) It will not be easy to measure the height that the ball bounces. Explain how taking the results 3 times at each height can make the evidence more reliable.
b) Here are 5 surfaces that a ball could bounce on:
carpet, concrete, wood, bed, grass.
Predict the order of what you think will be the highest to lowest bounce.
c) Then try it. Did you predict correctly?

2 Look again at Investigation 2.
a) Where would you put the zero mark of the ruler?
b) Scientists usually take at least 5 results in order to draw a line-graph. Explain why you think this is a good idea.

3 Look ahead to the next page, on Investigating. Read the left-hand page, and then choose one of the investigations. Plan it in detail so you are ready for the next lesson.

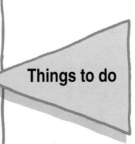

Things to do

Investigating by a fair test

In the last few lessons you have used several skills for doing science:

- **P**redicting
- **P**lanning an investigation
- **O**bserving
- **M**easuring
- **I**nterpreting and drawing conclusions
- **C**ommunicating your results
- **E**valuating.

The diagram shows how they link together for a fair test.

Sometimes the results of one investigation suggest a start for another investigation.

On the opposite page are suggestions for 3 investigations.

▶ Read them carefully. Then choose **one** of them (one that you haven't done before).

▶ Then **plan** it in detail (using this diagram). When your teacher has checked your plan, go ahead and do the investigation.

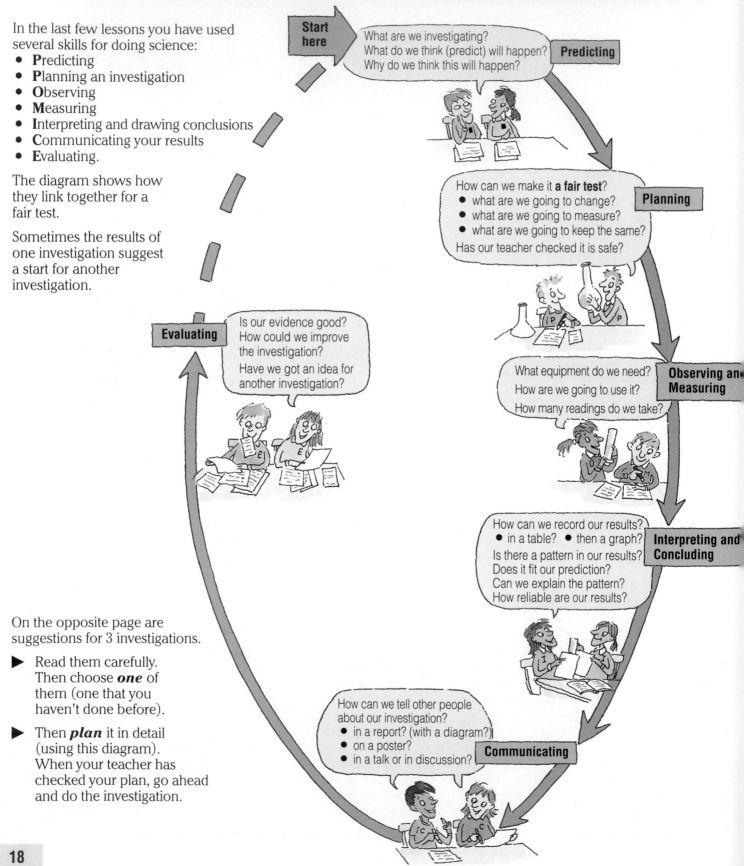

Start here

What are we investigating?
What do we think (predict) will happen?
Why do we think this will happen?

Predicting

How can we make it **a fair test**?
- what are we going to change?
- what are we going to measure?
- what are we going to keep the same?

Has our teacher checked it is safe?

Planning

What equipment do we need?
How are we going to use it?
How many readings do we take?

Observing and Measuring

How can we record our results?
- in a table? • then a graph?
Is there a pattern in our results?
Does it fit our prediction?
Can we explain the pattern?
How reliable are our results?

Interpreting and Concluding

How can we tell other people about our investigation?
- in a report? (with a diagram?)
- on a poster?
- in a talk or in discussion?

Communicating

Is our evidence good?
How could we improve the investigation?

Have we got an idea for another investigation?

Evaluating

1. Getting soaked

Paper towels are often used in kitchens and washrooms.
What do you think makes a **good** paper towel?

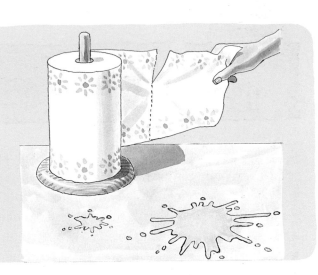

You will be given samples of 3 different paper towels,
labelled **A**, **B** and **C**.

Your job is to find out which of the towels is best at soaking up water.

Which towel would you recommend to a friend?

2. Tearing tissues

Television adverts for paper tissues often claim that they are
'strong even when wet'.
What do you think about this claim?

You will be given samples of 3 different makes of paper tissues,
labelled **X**, **Y** and **Z**.

Your job is to find out which of these tissues is strongest when wet.

Which tissue would you recommend to a friend?

3. Flaming Bunsens

Ben and Liz are arguing about Bunsen burners.

Ben says, "A burner with its air-hole fully open is always faster at
heating up water than two burners with their holes half-open."

Liz disagrees, "Two burners are always faster because they use up
more gas."

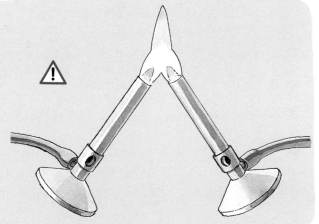

What do you think?

How can you find out safely?

---

1 When you have done your investigation
think about how you could make it better.
You are **evaluating** it.
Write down your ideas (and draw diagrams
if they will help to explain).

2 Choose one of the other investigations
(one that you haven't done before).
Plan it in detail.

Things to do

Other ways of investigating

As well as 'fair test' investigations, there are other ways of doing a scientific enquiry. As a scientist, you can:

- Collect data from books, ROMs or the Internet.
- Identify and classify living things, rocks or chemicals.
- Study how things change over time: the moon or a baby.
- Invent and make something to solve a scientific problem.
- Collect data about things that happen around us, and then **look for patterns** to explain them.

Looking for patterns

In these enquiries you have all sorts of natural variables. You cannot control them, so you cannot do a fair-test investigation. But you can still use your investigative skills.

Woodlice in the wild

Amy, Luke and Calum are in the garden, looking at woodlice, as you can see in the picture:

Amy said, "They are not under this dry stone."
Luke said, "Perhaps they like to be out in the open."

Calum wanted to investigate.
He said, "I think that we will find more under wet things than under dry things or out in the open."

Luke said, "Let's choose different places and count how many woodlice are in each place."

Then Amy said, "Use an equal area each time you count them. Or measure your whole area, and then work out the number in 100 cm^2"

When they had finished, they put their results in a table:

▶ Look at what the 3 students said, and find:

a a question **b** a hypothesis, **c** a prediction,
d an observation, and **e** a piece of planning.

f From the results, what can you conclude about where woodlice like to be?

g Does the evidence match Calum's hypothesis and his prediction?

h Make a prediction about what woodlice do when they are out in the light.

i Luke wrote this evaluation. What do you think is good (or bad) about it?

Place	Number of woodlice per 100 cm^2
Under a wet stone	69
Under bark of a dead tree	47
On a path	4
Under a smooth dry stone	0
Under wet leaves on soil	29
Amongst grass	5
Under a flower pot	32

There are some things we could not control: the wetness of the wet places, the temperature, other animals.
I think we can trust our conclusion because there was a big difference in the numbers we found in the wet and dry places. We could look in more places. We could look for different kinds of woodlice in different places.

Charles Darwin was a scientist. In 1831 he went on a voyage:

GALAPAGOS ISLANDS

Equator

PACIFIC OCEAN

We're going to sail round the world on a survey.

HMS BEAGLE

Darwin travelled for 5 years. Everywhere he went, he **collected** plants, animals and fossils.

On the Galapagos Islands he found giant tortoises:

This is interesting — the tortoise shells are different on each island. I wonder why?

Charles **observed**, and looked for **patterns**. He found that each island had its own species of finches (a bird). There were 13 species of finches, and …

…. each has a different beak!

Charles looked for more **evidence** and found a **pattern**. He found each species of finch ate a different food.

large seed eater

small seed eater

insect eater

fruit eater

Perhaps the species had **changed** to suit the food on each island**?**

He found lots more **evidence** on his voyage. Back home, Darwin worked for 20 years to **draw conclusions**.

I think all the species have changed, over a very long time. They change to suit their environment.

… and the human species has changed as well!

Darwin and another scientist, Alfred Wallace, announced their 'Theory of Evolution' in 1858.

Darwin wrote a famous book:

The Origin of Species 1859

People were shocked at these new ideas.

Nowadays we have much more evidence, and most people believe Darwin was right.

1 In the story above, some words are emphasised: *collected, observed, pattern, evidence, draw conclusions.* Explain what each one means, and why it is important in an investigation.

2 Use a book, a ROM or the Internet to:
a) Find out more about Darwin's life, *or*
b) Find out more about his book, *or*
c) Find out why "People were shocked at these new ideas."

Things to do

Questions

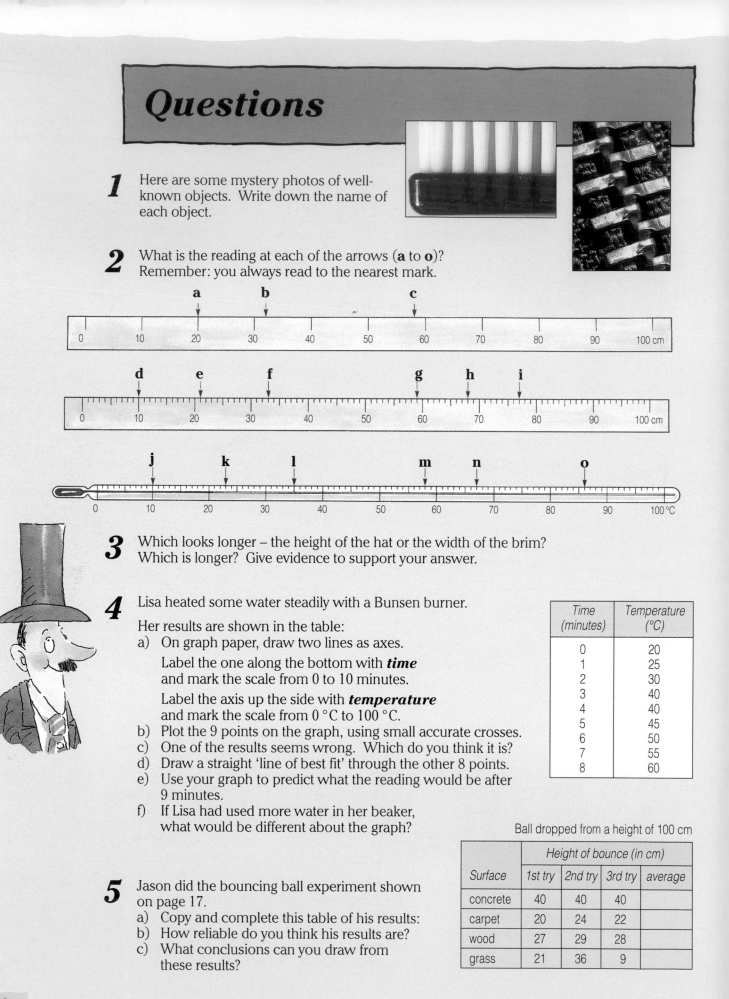

1 Here are some mystery photos of well-known objects. Write down the name of each object.

2 What is the reading at each of the arrows (**a** to **o**)?
Remember: you always read to the nearest mark.

3 Which looks longer – the height of the hat or the width of the brim?
Which is longer? Give evidence to support your answer.

4 Lisa heated some water steadily with a Bunsen burner.

Her results are shown in the table:
a) On graph paper, draw two lines as axes.

   Label the one along the bottom with **time**
   and mark the scale from 0 to 10 minutes.

   Label the axis up the side with **temperature**
   and mark the scale from 0 °C to 100 °C.
b) Plot the 9 points on the graph, using small accurate crosses.
c) One of the results seems wrong. Which do you think it is?
d) Draw a straight 'line of best fit' through the other 8 points.
e) Use your graph to predict what the reading would be after 9 minutes.
f) If Lisa had used more water in her beaker, what would be different about the graph?

Time (minutes)	Temperature (°C)
0	20
1	25
2	30
3	40
4	40
5	45
6	50
7	55
8	60

5 Jason did the bouncing ball experiment shown on page 17.
a) Copy and complete this table of his results:
b) How reliable do you think his results are?
c) What conclusions can you draw from these results?

Ball dropped from a height of 100 cm

Surface	Height of bounce (in cm)			
	1st try	2nd try	3rd try	average
concrete	40	40	40	
carpet	20	24	22	
wood	27	29	28	
grass	21	36	9	

Making and using materials

Everything around us is made of materials. Some are found naturally. Some need to be made from raw materials.

You need to choose the right material for the right job.

What would your life be like without …
wood, oil, glass, plastic, metals … ?

In this topic:
2a *Looking at materials*
2b *What's in a material?*
2c *Making new materials*
2d *Using materials*

Looking at materials

▶ Look at some of the words we use to describe materials.

• In your group, choose one of the words. You need to explain to other groups what the word means.
BUT … You cannot use the word itself!
    You cannot use the opposite of the word!

• Write down an explanation of your chosen word on a piece of paper. You can also draw pictures to give clues.

If there is time you can do this with other words from the list.

• Now swap pieces of paper with other groups.
Look at the explanations and pictures.
Try to guess what the words are.

If you think that other groups have good explanations, make a note of them. This may be useful for **Things to do** question 2.

Soft weak **HARD** smooth soluble Rough flexible Stretchy shiny **STRONG** DULL

Properties of materials

As you have already discovered, each material has its own set of **properties**. You have been using words which describe properties. For example, the properties of rubber could be:

it is smooth, it is dull, it is flexible and it is stretchy.

Remember that a **property** must describe **any** piece of the material.

▶ Think about the materials chosen for the items in these photographs.

For each one, write down at least 2 properties which make it a suitable material.

What a disaster!

There will be some disasters here!

▶ Look at these pictures of materials in use in 4 different situations.

In each case say why the material shown is not suitable.

Suggest a better material for use in each case.

A What do you think about concrete shoes?

B Have you ever driven across a rubber bridge?

C Do you have wooden pans at home?

D Would you like a steel pillow?

How strong?

Plywood is made of a few thin sheets of wood glued together.
Ann says "Plywood can't be as strong as one solid piece of wood".
How could you test Ann's idea?
Write a plan for your test.
How could you make your results reliable?

Things to do

1 Give 2 examples in each case of materials which are:
a) strong b) flexible c) soft.

2 You can make your own properties dictionary.
Write a list of 10 words used to describe materials.
Put the words in alphabetical order.
Write a sentence to explain the meaning of each word.
Draw pictures if this helps you to explain.

3 Make a simple drawing of a bicycle.
Add labels to show the materials used to make the various parts.

4 Write down 3 uses of each of these materials:
a) wood
b) plastic
c) metal
d) glass
e) concrete.

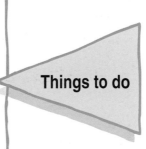

5 Do a survey of the ways in which food is packaged. Look at home or in a shop to see what types of containers are used.
a) What materials are used for the packaging?
b) Why are these materials suitable?
c) Do you think all the packaging is always needed?

What's in a material?

The ancient Greeks thought that all substances were made up of 4 things:

- earth
- air
- fire
- water.

They thought that these things were joined together in different amounts to make different materials.

▶ Do you agree with this idea?

Discuss it in your group.

Look at the photographs of structures from Lego.
Lego pieces are simple blocks which can be combined in different ways.
The same blocks can be made into many different objects.

In the same way all the materials used in the world are made from simple substances.
These simple substances can be combined in different ways to make different materials.

In 1661 Robert Boyle gave a name to the simplest substances.
He called them **elements**.
Scientists still use this description.

An element is a substance which cannot be broken down into anything simpler.

You will find out more about elements in Books 8 and 9.

There are over 100 elements. 92 of these are found naturally on Earth.
The same elements can combine in different ways.
Many different materials can be made.
The elements carbon, hydrogen and oxygen can combine to make sugar or to make the acid in vinegar.

Naming materials

Look at the objects on display. They are made from different materials.
How many of these materials do you know?
List the names of as many as possible.

Most of the materials are made from elements combined together.
Some are made from **only one** element.

Can you guess which objects on display are made from **only one element?**
Can you name the element in each case?
Write down your ideas.

Combining elements

You are going to combine two elements – magnesium and oxygen (from the air).

a What does the magnesium look like?

b What does the oxygen look like?

Stand a Bunsen burner on a heat-resistant mat.
Light the burner. Then make the air-hole half open.
Get a short piece of magnesium ribbon from your teacher.
Hold it at arm's length in some tongs.
Move the magnesium ribbon into the flame (do not look directly at it).

Observe what happens.

Magnesium has now combined with the oxygen.

c What does the new material look like?

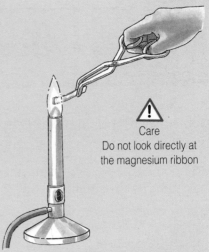

⚠️ Care
Do not look directly at
the magnesium ribbon

Magnesium combines with oxygen
in the air. It makes a new material.

Removing elements

Copper carbonate is made from the elements copper, carbon and oxygen.
Put 4 spatula measures of copper carbonate in a test-tube.
Heat it with a normal Bunsen burner flame.

Observe what happens.

d What did the copper carbonate look like at the start?
e What does the substance look like at the end?

The copper carbonate *loses* something during the heating.
It loses some carbon and some oxygen.

f Where do you think these elements have gone? Try to explain.

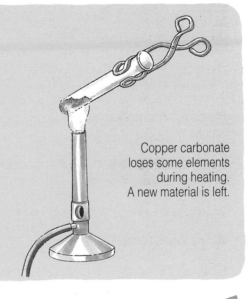

Copper carbonate
loses some elements
during heating.
A new material is left.

Things to do

1 Copy and complete using the words in the box.

element	combined	carbon
oxygen	copper	100

a) A substance which cannot be broken down into anything simpler is an . . . .
b) All substances are made from elements . . . . in different ways.
c) There are more than . . . . elements.
d) Copper carbonate is made of 3 elements:
. . . ., ... and . . . .

2 Which of these substances are elements?
copper, carbon dioxide, oxygen, iron, sodium chloride, tin, magnesium, magnesium oxide, copper carbonate?

3 Sometimes when elements combine, it's bad news.
What happens to iron when it combines with oxygen in damp weather?
Write about the problems caused by this.

Making new materials

Some materials are **natural**. Others are **made**.

All these materials are made from **elements**.

Sometimes the elements are already combined in nature to give us a useful material.

The wool from a sheep is a **natural** material.
Why is it useful**?**

The wood from a tree is a **natural** material.
Why is it useful**?**

Sometimes scientists combine the elements in new ways.
This is to make a useful material. The material is **synthetic**.

Glass is a **synthetic** material.
It can be made from sand and sodium carbonate.

Just the job!

Some of the clothes you wear are made from natural materials. Examples are cotton, wool and silk.
Other clothes are made from **synthetic** (made) materials. Examples are polyester and acrylic.
You may have some clothes made of a mixture of materials. An example is polyester and cotton.

Different materials have different properties. Look at the pictures here. For each one, say which properties the material used for the clothing should have.

Example:
Ideally T-shirts should be made of material which is light and lets body heat out.

When you buy a piece of clothing you need to think about how you will use it. The type of material may be important.

Maybe you want to be ... just fashionable,
　　　　　　　　　　　　... warm,
　　　　　　　　　　　　... dry**?**

In the next investigation you can compare 2 different materials used to make clothes.

Comparing a natural and a synthetic material

Your teacher will give you a sample of 2 materials. One of these is natural. The other is synthetic.

In your group plan an investigation to compare the materials. You could design tests to see which material will ...

or 　(a)　keep you drier
　　　(b)　keep you warmer.

Choose one of the ideas.

flammable

Make a prediction, then plan a fair test.

Look back to page 16 if you need help to do this.

Write down your plan.

You need to include details of:
- the apparatus you will need
- what you will do (include safety points)
- what measurements or observations you will make
- how you will make your results reliable
- how you will present your results.

Your plan should be shown to your teacher before you start practical work.

If there is time, your teacher may let you plan and do another test.

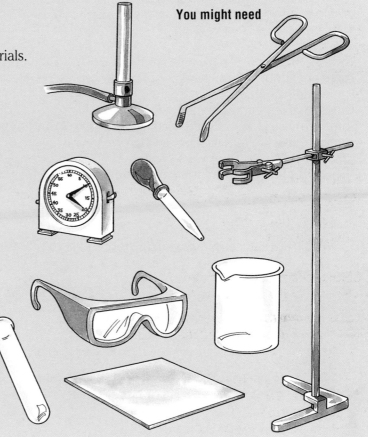
You might need

1　Copy the table into your book. Write down 3 materials in each column.

Natural	Synthetic (made)

2　Find out about the story of **either** cotton **or** silk.
Where is the material found?
Where is it made?
How is it changed for us to use?

3　Do a survey of your clothes at home.
- Look at the label to see what your clothes are made of.
- What does the material feel like? (soft, rough, smooth etc.)
- Are there any special care instructions, e.g. for washing or drying?

Record your findings in a table.
From your list say:
a)　which material can be washed at the highest temperature?
b)　which material feels the roughest?

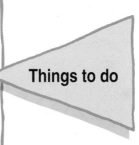
Things to do

2d Using materials

We use up lots of material every day.

▶ Think about what you have done since you got up this morning.
Make a list of all the things you've thrown away.
Could any of these things have been used again?
Do you recycle anything at home or at school?

There are about 7000 million people in the world today.
The world's population is growing.
The Earth's resources are being used up.
Some of these resources are used to make new **kinds** of materials.
Some are used to replace items which we throw away.

The Earth's resources are the **raw materials** from which we make other things.

▶ Look at the list of things we get from some raw materials.
In your group discuss whether we need these things.
Which substances are **essential** for us to survive? Which are not?

Substance from raw material	Raw material
salt	sea
oxygen	air
plastics	coal, crude oil, natural gas
copper	rocks
vegetable oil	living things (plants)

A scientific enquiry

Look at the Task Questions on the opposite page.
Choose 1 of these questions to investigate.
Carry out a scientific enquiry.

Think about:
- where you will get the information from (try to use more than one source)
- how you will present your findings (diagrams, tables, charts or graphs?).

Make sure that you:
- look at all the evidence and information
- make a conclusion (answer the question)
- consider whether your evidence is reliable (are you sure this is the right conclusion?).

Task Question   *Artificial fertiliser – friend or enemy?*

Carry out an enquiry to answer this question.

These are some of the questions you could answer to help your enquiry:

- What is a fertiliser?
- What are the raw materials used to make fertiliser?
- How are artificial fertilisers made?
- Why do we need artificial fertilisers?
- How much artificial fertiliser is used each year in the UK?
- How much does artificial fertiliser cost?
- What are the disadvantages of using artificial fertiliser?

Task Question   *Recycling – is it worth it?*

Carry out an enquiry to answer this question.

These are some of the questions you could answer to help your enquiry:

- What is recycling?
- Which materials are recycled in the UK?
- Why do people choose to recycle?
- What does the recycling process involve?
- How much does it cost to recycle materials?
- In the UK, what percentage of waste is recycled?
- Why isn't more waste recycled?

1   Some of the Earth's resources have many uses.
Crude oil is an important resource.
It is a mixture of many substances.
The percentage of each substance is shown in this table:

Name of substance in crude oil	% of substance in crude oil
fuel gas	2
petrol	6
naphtha	10
kerosine	13
diesel oil	19
fuel and bitumen	50

a)   Draw a bar-chart to show this information.
b)   Choose 4 of the substances found in crude oil. Draw pictures to show a use for each of them.

2   Look at the table of raw materials on the opposite page. Which of the 5 could be used to get:
a)   sugar?   c)   nitrogen?
b)   iron?   d)   pure water?

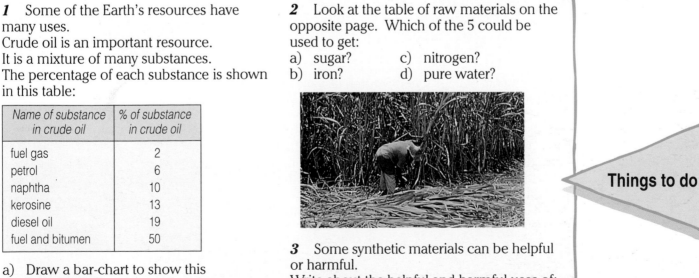

3   Some synthetic materials can be helpful or harmful.
Write about the helpful and harmful uses of:
a)   detergents
b)   medicines
c)   explosives.

Things to do

Questions

1 Choose one of the following materials:

> gold   paper   glass
>   wood   plastic

Collect pictures from newspapers and magazines to show your material in use in different objects.

2 Look at the picture of a playground and choose 6 objects which could be made from different materials.
Copy out this table and complete it for each of your objects.

Object	Material used to make it	Raw materials from which the material is made

3 Crude oil is an important raw material.
What do you know about crude oil?
Write down as many things as you can.

4 Mrs Walker is planning to decorate Neil's bedroom. Neil is two years old and messy!
Mrs Walker has 3 samples of wallpaper which the adverts say are 'easy to clean'.
 a) Plan an investigation to find out which wallpaper is the easiest to clean.
 b) What other factors might Mrs Walker consider before buying the paper?

5 The contents of your school wastebins have been surveyed.
The results are shown in the table. A group of pupils wants to find out if the waste can be recycled.
 a) Draw a bar-chart of these results.
 b) What percentage of the waste is plastic?
 c) Where do you think most of the waste aluminium came from?
 d) Do you think it's worth recycling materials?
 Why? Why not?
 e) How would you encourage pupils in school to recycle waste?

Type of waste	Number of items
paper	85
glass	45
aluminium	30
other metals	5
plastic	30
other	5

6 Think about the type of material used to make the drainpipes on a new house.
Make a list of the properties this material should have.

Energy

3

Without energy nothing can ever happen!

All living things need energy to stay alive and to move.
You get your energy from your food.

Machines cannot work without energy.
Our homes, transport and factories need the energy that
comes from fuels.

In this topic:

What is energy?

We often use the word '**energy**'.
Tina says, "I've got lots of energy today."
John says, "I haven't got enough energy to climb the hill."
A car-driver says, "I need some more petrol – my car has almost run out of energy."

▶ Write down three sentences of your own, using the word 'energy'.

▶ What do you think the word 'energy' means?
Where do you get your energy from?

▶ Look at the photograph. How many examples of energy can you find? Make a list.

Energy diagrams

Energy is needed to get jobs done, or make things work.
To get a job done, energy must be moved or **transferred** from one place to another.

Example 1
Suppose you wind up a clockwork toy, and then let it run across the table.
What are the energy transfers?

start
energy stored in your body → energy stored in the wound-up spring → movement energy of the toy

This is an **Energy Transfer Diagram**.

Example 2
Sometimes an Energy Transfer Diagram splits into two or more parts.
Suppose you switch on a torch:

energy stored in the battery → energy lighting up the room
energy heating up the bulb

The energy heating up the bulb is **wasted** energy. It is not useful.

Example 3
Rub your hands together quickly about 20 times.
What do you notice? Copy and complete this energy diagram:

. . . . stored in my . . . . → movement energy of my hands → energy . . . . up my hands
. . . . of the sound made by my hands

Energy transfers

Try each of these experiments and observe them carefully.
Think about the energy transfers. For each one:
- sketch a diagram of the equipment, and
- draw an Energy Transfer Diagram.

a a clockwork car

b a battery and a lamp bulb

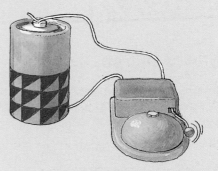

c a battery and a buzzer or door-bell

d a Bunsen burner

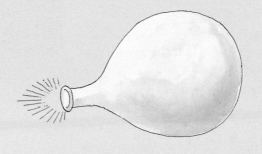

e blow up a balloon and then release it

f a dynamo and a lamp

Measuring energy

Sometimes we need to measure the amount of energy. The unit we use for measuring energy is the **joule**. This is written as **J** for short.

The joule is named after James Joule (1818–1889) who did many experiments on energy.

A joule is a small unit of energy. To lift an apple from the floor up on to a table needs about 1 joule of energy.

But if you *eat* the apple, it will give you a lot of energy – about 200 000 joules of energy. That's enough energy to walk up 50 flights of stairs!

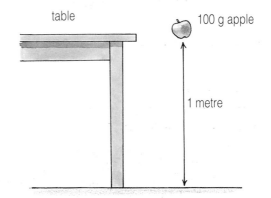

table   100 g apple

1 metre

---

1 Copy and complete:
a) . . . . is needed to get jobs done.
b) Energy is measured in . . . .

2 Draw a diagram to show the energy transfers when you pedal a bicycle.
Label it clearly.
How do you think it will change if you oil your bike?

3 Draw an Energy Transfer Diagram for a battery-powered television set.

4 Draw Energy Transfer Diagrams for:
a) a girl firing an arrow from a bow
b) a boy kicking a football
c) a bonfire burning
d) a firework rocket
e) a petrol-powered car.

Things to do

Go with energy

Stored energy

Energy can be stored.
For example, petrol has stored energy.
When petrol burns in a car, the stored energy
is transferred to movement energy of
the car **and** energy for heating the car:

Stored energy is often called **potential energy**.

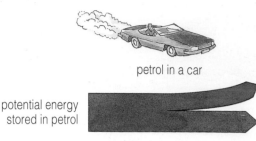

petrol in a car

potential energy
stored in petrol

energy heating up
the car and the air

movement energy
of the car

Here are some examples of stored energy:

- **Chemical energy**   For example: in petrol; in a battery; in
  the food that you eat.

- **Strain energy**   For example: in a catapult; in a clockwork car;
  in a balloon that has been blown up.

- **Gravitational energy**   For example: if you are at the top of
  a ladder, you have gravitational potential energy.
  If you fall off the ladder, the energy will damage you!

- Look at the photograph. What energy does the skier have at the
  top of the hill**?**

  When she skis down, this potential energy is transferred to her
  movement energy. (Another name for movement energy is
  kinetic energy.)

▶ Look back at experiments **a–f** on page 35.
  Where is the stored energy in each one**?**   Make a list.

potential energy ➡ kinetic energy

The energy law

Here is an energy diagram for a battery
connected to an electric motor:

If we measure the amount of energy (in
joules) **before** the transfer and **after** the
transfer, we find **it is the same amount**.

In the diagram, 100 joules of energy stored
in the battery is transferred to 70 joules of
movement energy and 30 joules of energy
heating up the motor.
So: 100 = 70 + 30, the same amount of energy.

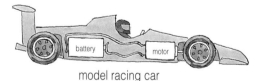

model racing car

100 J
potential energy
stored in the
battery

70 J
movement
energy

30 J
energy heating
up the motor
(wasted energy)

However, only 70 joules of energy are useful to us, as movement
energy. The other 30 J are wasted, because they are no use to us.

This is what usually happens in energy transfers.
**Although there is the same amount of energy afterwards,
not all of it is useful.**

A steam engine

Look carefully at a steam engine doing a job of work.

steam engine lifting a weight

steam engine

fuel

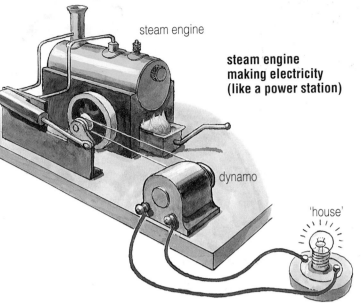

steam engine

steam engine making electricity (like a power station)

dynamo

'house'

▶ Observe each one carefully and look for energy transfers. Draw an Energy Transfer Diagram for each one. Try to include all of the energy changes.

Investigating a clockwork toy

Plan an investigation to see how the **distance travelled** by a clockwork toy depends on **how much it is wound up**.

- How will you measure the distance accurately?
- Will you wind it up in full-turn steps or half-turn steps?
- How will you ensure it is a **fair test**?
- How can you make your results more reliable?

Ask your teacher to check your plan. How can you improve it?

Things to do

1 Copy and complete:
a) Stored energy is also called . . . . energy.
b) This includes chemical . . . . , ... energy and . . . . energy.
c) An Energy . . . . Diagram shows us how the energy is . . . .
d) The amount of . . . . before the transfer is always . . . . to the amount of energy . . . . the transfer.

2 A battery is connected to a lamp bulb. Draw an Energy Transfer Diagram for this. While it is switched on, the battery gives out 100 joules of energy. If 80 J are heating up the room, how many joules are lighting the room?

3 Which of these two words could you use for each of these examples – **potential** (stored) energy or **kinetic** (movement) energy:
a) a can of petrol?
b) a car travelling down a road?
c) water at the very top of a waterfall?
d) water at the bottom of a waterfall?
e) a stretched bow with the arrow about to be released?
f) the arrow half-way to the target?
g) a rock at the top of a cliff?
h) the rock falling, half-way down?

4 Use the internet, or an encyclopedia, to find out about the life of James Joule.

Food for energy

You need energy for running, sitting, breathing and even for sleeping.
In fact, everything you do needs energy.

You get your energy from your food. The food you eat is your fuel.
Almost everything you eat contains energy.

Energy in food is measured in **kilojoules (kJ)**, where **1 kilojoule = 1000 joules**.

▶ Look at the potential energy in these foods.

a How much energy is there in a breakfast of cornflakes, yoghurt and a cup of tea?

b How much energy is there in a meal of chips and 2 sausage rolls?

cornflakes with milk
700 kJ

yoghurt
400 kJ

sausage roll
1500 kJ

chips
1000 kJ

tea, milk and sugar
200 kJ

How much energy?

The energy stored in foods is often shown on the label.
It is usually shown in kilojoules (**kJ**), and also in kilocalories (kcal).
(kcal is a unit of energy often used in slimming diets.)

▶ Look at these food labels.

c Why is the energy given for 100 grams of each food?

d Which of these foods has the lowest energy per 100 g?

e What happens if the food you eat contains more energy than you need?

HP Baked Beans are rich in fibre and protein and form a valuable part of a nutritious and well balanced diet.

HP Baked Beans in a rich tomato sauce. The full flavour of tomatoes combined with natural, wholesome beans make HP Baked Beans delicious hot or cold, at breakfast, lunch and dinner.

NUTRITION INFORMATION:	
100 g provides	
ENERGY	280 kJ/66 kcal
PROTEIN	5.0 g
CARBOHYDRATE	11.0 g
(of which sugars	5.0 g)
FAT	0.5 g
(of which saturates	0.1 g)
SODIUM	0.5 g
FIBRE	7.3 g

FREE FROM
ARTIFICIAL COLOURS
AND PRESERVATIVES

HP Foods Limited, Market Harborough, Leics LE16 9BQ, England

NUTRITION
Sainsbury's Sardines in Brine are a good source of Calcium and Vitamin D, both needed for strong bones and teeth; Vitamin B_{12}, required for healthy blood and nervous system, Niacin which helps food to give us energy.

	TYPICAL VALUES PER 100 g (3½ oz) OF DRAINED PRODUCT
ENERGY	170 kCALORIES
	705 kJOULES
PROTEIN	23.4 g
CARBOHYDRATE	less than 0.1 g
TOTAL FAT	8.3 g
ADDED SALT	0.5 g
VITAMINS/ MINERALS	% OF RECOMMENDED DAILY AMOUNT
NIACIN	45%
VITAMIN B_{12}	1400%
VITAMIN D	300%
CALCIUM	110%
IRON	25%

Kellogg's
CRUNCHY NUT CORN FLAKES ®

THE BEST TO YOU

NUTRITION INFORMATION	Per 100 g	
ENERGY	1700	kJ
	400	kcal
PROTEIN	7.0	g
CARBOHYDRATE	83	g
of which sugars 35g		
starch 48 g		
FAT	4.0	g
of which saturates 0.8 g		
SODIUM	0.8	g
FIBRE	1.0	g
VITAMINS:		
NIACIN	16	mg
VITAMIN B_6	1.8	mg
RIBOFLAVIN (B_2)	1.5	mg
THIAMIN (B_1)	1.0	mg
FOLIC ACID	250	µg
VITAMIN D	2.8	µg
VITAMIN B_{12}	1.7	µg
IRON	6.7	mg

Investigating the energy in food

One way of measuring the amount of energy in some food is to burn it.

As the food burns, it gives out energy. We can use this energy to heat up some water.

The more energy stored in the food, the more energy is released and the hotter the water gets.

Plan an investigation to compare the energy content of a peanut with that of a pea.

- What apparatus will you need?
- What measurements will you take?
- How will you record your results?

Remember you must make it a **fair test**, and work safely.

When you have had your plan checked by your teacher, go ahead and do the investigation.

What do you find?

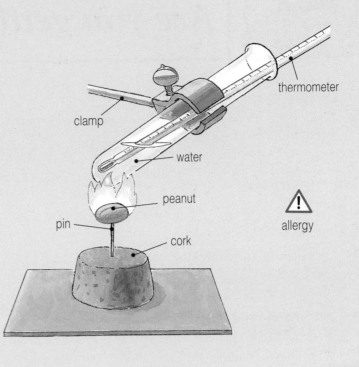

thermometer
clamp
water
peanut
pin
cork
allergy

---

1 For the next 24 hours, keep a record of all the food that you eat.
Next lesson you can use this to work out how much energy you have taken in.

2 Make a survey of how much energy is in different foods. Look at the food labels on packets and cans at home. List them under 'high energy food' or 'low energy food'.

3 Look at the bar-chart.
It shows the energy content in kilojoules for one gram of each food.
a) Which food gives the most energy?
b) Which two foods give the least energy?
c) Which foods would you take with you on a long walk in the mountains?
d) Which foods would make a good meal for someone who wants to lose weight?
e) How much energy would you get from 1 gram of bread?
f) How much energy would you get from 2 grams of carrot?

4 In your investigation, did all the energy from the peanut go to the water?
Was it a fair test?
What could you do to improve your investigation?

Things to do

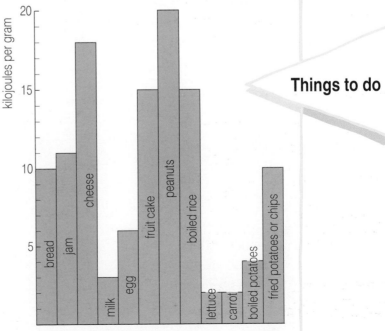

kilojoules per gram

bread, jam, cheese, milk, egg, fruit cake, peanuts, boiled rice, lettuce, carrot, boiled potatoes, fried potatoes or chips

3d *Are you getting enough energy?*

Think of the ways in which your body uses up energy.

▶ Make a list of things you have done today which have used up some of your energy.

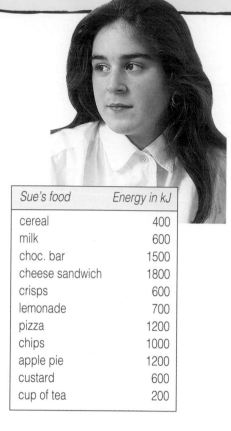

Energy intake

Sue is a 12-year old girl. The average energy needed by a girl her age is 9700 kJ per day.

▶ Look at Sue's meals for the last 24 hours and answer these questions.

a Work out Sue's total energy intake for the day (in kJ).

b Did Sue get enough energy for a girl of her age?

c Which 5 foods gave her most energy?

d What do you think would happen if her energy intake was much lower than 9700 kJ per day? How would this make her feel when she needed to be active?

Sue's food	Energy in kJ
cereal	400
milk	600
choc. bar	1500
cheese sandwich	1800
crisps	600
lemonade	700
pizza	1200
chips	1000
apple pie	1200
custard	600
cup of tea	200

How much energy

▶ Now work out your energy intake for the food you ate during 24 hours.
Use this table to find the energy content of each food, in kilojoules (kJ).

Average portion	kJ	Average portion	kJ	Average portion	kJ
red meat	2000	cornflakes	400	apple	200
chicken	900	milk (1 cup)	600	apple pie	1200
beefburger	1700	yoghurt	400	banana	300
lamb curry	1200	cheese	900	orange	200
pizza	1200	peas	300	chapatti	900
sausages	1500	tomatoes	100	bread (1 slice)	400
fish fingers	700	cabbage	80	pat of butter	200
spaghetti	500	carrots	80	jam	400
rice (boiled)	500	lettuce	40	cake (1 slice)	700
potatoes, boiled	400	choc. bar	1500	cola	600
chips	1000	ice cream	500	coffee	100
baked beans	400	crisps	600	sugar (teaspoon)	100
egg, boiled	400	jelly	300	squash	300
fried	500	biscuit	400	thick soup	600

e Did you eat enough to cover your energy needs?
(12-year-old girl = about 9700 kJ per day;
12-year-old boy = about 11 700 kJ per day)

f What advice would you give someone who is overweight about:
i) taking in less energy?
ii) using up more energy?

Different energy needs

The amount of energy that you need depends on:
- how big you are,
- how active you are,
- how fast you are growing.

▶ Look at the pictures and then answer these questions:

g Why do you think that males usually need more energy than females?

h Why do manual workers need more energy than office workers? How much more energy?

i Why does a 13-year-old boy need more energy than a male office worker? How much more does he need?

j Why does pregnancy increase a woman's energy needs?

boy 12-15 years
11 700 kJ/day

male manual worker
15 000 kJ/day

female office worker
9800 kJ/day

girl 12-15 years
9700 kJ/day

male office worker
11 000 kJ/day

pregnant woman
10 000 kJ/day

Energy intakes in different countries

▶ Look at the bar-chart:

k Which of these countries eats the most energy foods per person?

l Which country eats the least?

m Why do you think there are such large differences?
How will this affect the people's health?
Discuss these questions within your group.

kJ
energy eaten per person per day

14 000
12 000
10 000
8 000
6 000
4 000
2 000

Haiti · India · China · Japan · Brazil · U.K. · France · U.S.A.

---

1 Draw a bar-chart to show the energy needed per minute for these activities:

sleeping	4 kJ per minute
eating	6 kJ per minute
writing	7 kJ per minute
walking	15 kJ per minute
climbing stairs	20 kJ per minute
running	30 kJ per minute

2 Use the data in the table on the opposite page to plan:
a) a meal to give you about 3500 kJ
b) a day's diet for a female office worker who wants to lose weight
c) a day's diet for a male distance-runner in training for a race.

3 Make a survey of your class to find out what they eat for lunch.
Can you see any pattern in your results?

4 Find out about the dangers of slimming too much. What are **anorexia** and **bulimia**?

5 Plan an investigation to find out which foods birds prefer.

6 Use the internet or your school intranet to search for information about "world energy consumption" or "world energy resources". Write a brief report about the most important piece of information that you find. Explain why you think it is important.

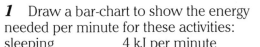

Things to do

Running out of energy

We need energy for running our homes, transport and factories. Most of this energy comes from burning **fuels**.
Fuels store energy.

▶ Make a list of all the fuels you can think of. The picture will help you.

▶ Write down 3 things about your life that would be different if we did not have these fuels.

Coal, oil and natural gas are called **fossil fuels**. They were made from plants and animals that lived on Earth about 100 million years ago.

▶ Look at the table of data and interpret it to answer these questions:

a Which fuel is easiest to set alight**?**

b Which fuel burns most cleanly**?**

c Which fossil fuel is a solid**?**

d Which is the liquid that gives us petrol**?**

e Which fuel gives most energy when 1 gram of it is burned**?**

f The price of these fuels varies from year to year, but from the table which is the cheapest**?**

Fossil fuel	Easy to light?	Burns cleanly?	Amount of energy released	Approx. amount of energy for £1
natural gas	very easy	yes	55 kJ per gram	230 000 kJ
oil	yes	no	45 kJ per gram	250 000 kJ
coal	no	no	30 kJ per gram	300 000 kJ

Fossil fuels are **non-renewable** sources of energy. Once we have used them up, they are gone for ever!

▶ On the time-chart find:
  • the year you were born
  • where we are now
  • the year when you will be 40 years old
  • the year in which you will be 60.

g From this chart, what do you notice about the fuels**?**

h What can you predict about your life when you are 60**?**

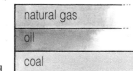

natural gas
oil
coal

1980　2000　2020　2040　2060　2080　2100　2120　2140　2160　2180　2200　2220　2240

▶ There are other sources of energy called **renewable** sources. For example: energy from the wind (as in a windmill).

i How many other renewable sources of energy can you name**?** Make a list.

Energy consumption

Fossil fuels are used in some power stations to make electricity.

We can also get energy from:
- **nuclear power stations**. They use uranium but this is getting scarce.
- **hydro-electric power stations**. They use the potential energy from water stored in high dams.
- **biomass**. This is the energy stored in growing plants, such as wood.

▶ Look at the pie-charts and interpret them to answer these questions:

j List the energy sources used in the UK.

k What was the percentage for natural gas in the UK? Where do you use natural gas in school?

l Which were the biggest sources of energy for the UK in 2000?

m Which was the smallest source of energy for the UK? Why is this?

n Which source was not used in the UK?

o Which of the sources are **renewable**?

p In your group, compare the two charts and suggest some reasons why you think they are different.

q *Predict* what you think the world pie-chart will look like when you are 60.

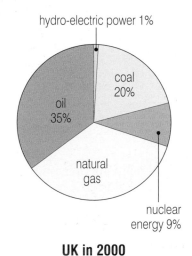

UK in 2000

hydro-electric power 1%
coal 20%
oil 35%
natural gas
nuclear energy 9%

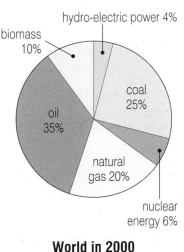

World in 2000

hydro-electric power 4%
biomass 10%
coal 25%
oil 35%
natural gas 20%
nuclear energy 6%

High tea

Imagine you are climbing a high mountain.
You will need to heat some snow, to make some soup or tea.

You can take with you either a **candle** or a **spirit-burner**, to heat the snow.

Plan an investigation to find out which is better.

- Sketch the equipment you would use.

- How will you make your investigation safe to do?

---

1 Petrol, coal and potatoes are fuels. Explain how you could use each of these fuels to keep you warm.

2 Make a survey of all the fuels used in your home.

3 Draw a poster advertisement to promote a fuel. Choose one of these: oil, gas, wood or coal.

4 Make a table showing how people could save fossil fuels. For example:

Action to be taken	How it saves fuel
Drive smaller cars	Uses less petrol

5 Make a list of the properties of an **ideal** fuel.

Things to do

Questions

1 Draw Energy Transfer Diagrams for:
a)   a coal fire
b)   a box being lifted up on to a shelf
c)   an archer pulling back a bow-string and then releasing it.

2 Make a list of 6 things that use energy in your home. Put them in order from the one you think uses the most energy to the one that uses the least.

3 Make a list of the ways that your school could reduce its energy bills.

4 About one-third of all the people on Earth do not get enough to eat.
a)   Why do you think this is? Give as many possible reasons as you can.
b)   What do you think should be done to solve this problem?

5 Advertisements for some HP2 torch batteries claim that they have more energy than others.
Plan an investigation to find out which of two new batteries has more energy stored.

6 Explain why the following fuels are good for the jobs they do:
a)   sugar in a cup of tea
b)   petrol in a car
c)   gas in a Bunsen burner
d)   wax in a candle
e)   coal in a power station.

7 The energy sources that each country chooses to use depend upon:
i)   economic reasons (price, availability, etc.)
ii)   environmental reasons (pollution, damage to the landscape, etc.)

Think carefully about these reasons, and then list the advantages and disadvantages for your country, of using:
a)   coal
b)   hydroelectric power
c)   wind power

8 Write about all the energy transfers you can see in the photograph.

The variety of life

4

Have you ever been down to the seashore?
It's an interesting and exciting place to visit.

Many creatures live there, especially in rock-pools.
Rock-pools are left behind when the tide goes out.
Each is like a small aquarium. Many plants and animals
survive in rock-pools until the tide returns.

Next time you go to the seashore, have a look to see how
many animals and plants you can find.
But be sure not to damage them. Leave them
undisturbed so that other people can look at them.

oyster catcher

Coral weed

mussels

Enteromorpha weed

toothed wrack

sea urchin

goby

limpets

shore crab

whelk

prawn

hermit crab

winkle

ragworm

sea anemones

barnacles

starfish

In this topic:
4a *Alive or not?*
4b *Putting living things into groups*
4c *On safari!*
4d *It's a green world*
4e *Life's building blocks*
4f *Getting ORGANised!*

45

Alive or not?

How can you tell if something is alive or not**?**

▶ Write down as many ideas as you can about what **all** living things do.
Discuss whether your ideas are true for each of the following:
  • rabbit
  • table
  • tree
  • robot
  • cheese

▶ The table below shows some more ideas about being alive.
The non-living thing in the table is a car engine.
The living thing can be an animal of your choice.
It could be you!

Draw the table and answer the questions.
The first one is done for you.

	Animal (living)	Car engine (non-living)
Does it need air?	yes	yes
Does it move?		
Can it grow?		
Does it need food (fuel)?		
Can it feed on its own?		
Does it give out waste?		
Can it feel things?		
Will it die when it is old?		
Can it be a parent?		
Can it be eaten by another living thing?		

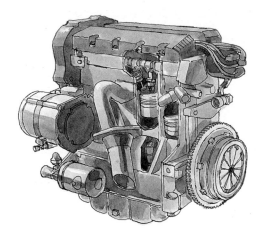

Energy matters

In the previous topic you found that to stay alive living things need energy. Can you remember where living things get their energy from**?**

Sugar is a food that gives us a lot of energy.
Sugar is broken down inside animals and plants to get the energy out.
We call this **respiration**.

SUGAR + OXYGEN = CARBON DIOXIDE + WATER + ENERGY FOR LIFE

Oxygen is needed for respiration to take place.
When sugar burns in oxygen it releases energy.
What else do you think is produced**?**

Explorations Unlimited

Dear Scientists,

One of our expeditions has found something interesting in Death Valley. They are not sure, but they may have found some very rare seeds. We want to know whether they are alive or not?

Please plan and carry out an investigation to find out if the seeds are living or not. Remember to make it a fair test and send me your report.

Thanks

Des Covery

Plants: the green machines

Do you know what plants can do that most other living things can't?

They can make their own food by a process called **photosynthesis**. In their leaves they have a green substance called **chlorophyll**. With this they can use energy from sunlight to make sugars.

Differences between plants and animals

▶ Copy and complete this table to show the main differences between these 2 types of living things.

Plants	Animals
1. Don't move around much	1. Move around a lot
2.	2.

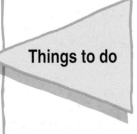
Things to do

1 There are some robots that can move and that are sensitive to such things as smells and sounds.
Why do we say they are not alive?

2 Do you know of any plants that provide food for humans as a result of photosynthesis? Make a list and say which part of the plant you think is eaten, e.g. root, leaf, seed, etc.

3 Copy out the activities listed in the left-hand column, then match each with the correct example from the right-hand column:

GROWING   escaping from danger
RESPIRING   becoming a parent
GETTING RID OF WASTE   increasing your body size
MOVING   smelling food
REPRODUCING   having a snack
FEEDING   going to the loo
USING SENSES   using up energy in a race

Putting living things into groups

There are millions of different kinds of plants and animals in the world.

▶ Make a list of 10 animals by yourself.

Compare your list with others in your group.

Each different kind of plant and animal is called a **species**. You have listed 10 species of animal.

Over the years scientists have tried to give every species of plant and animal a name of its own.

▶ Why do you think this has been difficult?

It has been made easier by putting similar living things into groups.
This is called **classification**.

▶ The 2 biggest groups are plants and animals. What decides whether a living thing is a plant or an animal?

To make it even easier to identify living things we break the big groups into smaller groups.

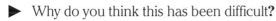

Living things → Animals → Vertebrates (have backbones) / Invertebrates (no backbones); Plants → Flowering / Non-flowering

▶ Which of the groups in the diagram above do you belong to?

▶ How many vertebrates can your group name in one minute?

Invertebrates (animals without backbones)

Jellyfish and sea anemones Jelly-like body. Have tentacles with stinging cells to catch food

Flatworms Flattened body with no segments

Roundworms Long thin body with no segments

Segmented worms Long, tube-shaped body made of segments

Molluscs Many have a shell. Body not in segments. Move around on a muscular foot

Starfish and sea urchin 5 'arms' or star-shaped pattern on their bodies. Spiny skins

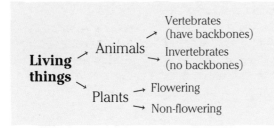

Arthropods Jointed legs. Body has a hard outer skeleton

The arthropods are a group of invertebrates w jointed legs. They can be divided into 4 smalle groups:

Arthropods

Crustaceans ('cru-stations') Chalky outer skeleton. Most live in water

Insects 6 legs. 3 parts to the body. Have wings

Spiders 8 legs. 2 parts to the body. No wings

Centipedes and milliped Long body made up of segments. Many legs

▶ Look back at the picture of the rock-pool on page 45.

a There are many invertebrates in the picture. Use the information on this page to decide which group each belongs to.

b The goby and the oystercatcher are vertebrates. To which group do you think each belongs?

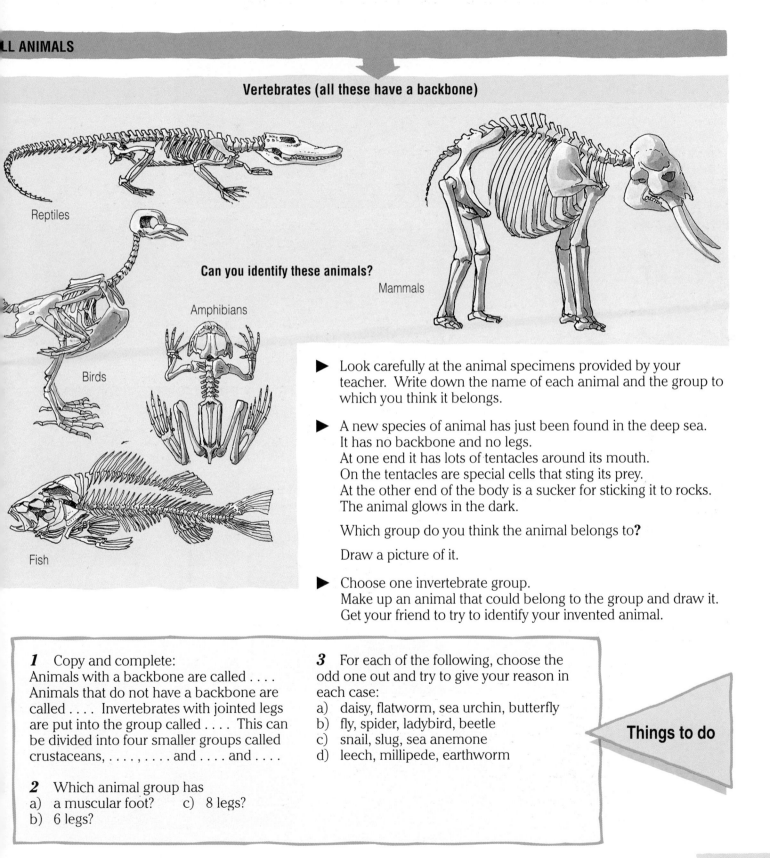

Vertebrates (all these have a backbone)

Reptiles

Can you identify these animals?

Mammals

Amphibians

Birds

Fish

▶ Look carefully at the animal specimens provided by your teacher. Write down the name of each animal and the group to which you think it belongs.

▶ A new species of animal has just been found in the deep sea.
It has no backbone and no legs.
At one end it has lots of tentacles around its mouth.
On the tentacles are special cells that sting its prey.
At the other end of the body is a sucker for sticking it to rocks.
The animal glows in the dark.

Which group do you think the animal belongs to?

Draw a picture of it.

▶ Choose one invertebrate group.
Make up an animal that could belong to the group and draw it.
Get your friend to try to identify your invented animal.

1 Copy and complete:
Animals with a backbone are called . . . .
Animals that do not have a backbone are called . . . . Invertebrates with jointed legs are put into the group called . . . . This can be divided into four smaller groups called crustaceans, ... , ... and . . . . and . . . .

2 Which animal group has
a) a muscular foot?   c) 8 legs?
b) 6 legs?

3 For each of the following, choose the odd one out and try to give your reason in each case:
a) daisy, flatworm, sea urchin, butterfly
b) fly, spider, ladybird, beetle
c) snail, slug, sea anemone
d) leech, millipede, earthworm

Things to do

On safari!

Hi, my name's Lizzie. Last Saturday I went to the Wildlife Park with my friend Richard. We saw llamas with their young. It was a hot day to have such hairy coats. Next we saw a family of baboons. They were very hairy and one mother was feeding its baby. I remembered that **mammals** feed their young on milk. In a different part of the park we saw zebras and camels.

After a stop for drinks at the cafe, we walked to the **reptile** house. There were lizards and snakes from many different countries. We were able to hold the boa constrictor and we could feel its dry skin covered with scales.

We also saw some frogs, toads and salamanders. These had smooth, moist skin and a label said that they were called **amphibians**.

We went to the **bird** house next.
Here there were some very rare birds.
We saw California condors and whooping cranes.
They are in danger because the places where they live are being destroyed.
A bird of paradise had beautiful feathers.

We couldn't leave before seeing the aquarium.
There were many types of **fish** in freshwater and seawater tanks.
There were tunny, wrasse and bream as well as perch and roach.
They all had scaly skin and fins for swimming.

On the way home Richard and I talked about all the animals that we had seen. Later that day, I opened my science book at the page 'Vertebrates: animals with backbones'.

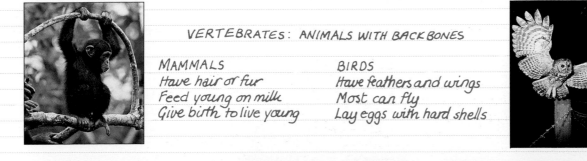

VERTEBRATES: ANIMALS WITH BACKBONES

MAMMALS
Have hair or fur
Feed young on milk
Give birth to live young

BIRDS
Have feathers and wings
Most can fly
Lay eggs with hard shells

REPTILES
Have dry, scaly skin
Lay eggs with soft shells

AMPHIBIANS
Have smooth, moist skin
Breed in water

FISH
Live all of the time in water
Swim using fins
Breathe using gills
Have scaly skin

► Copy out this table.

Mammals	Birds	Reptiles	Amphibians	Fish
Llamas				

Read through the story and write down the name of each animal mentioned in the correct column of your table.

► Write down 3 reasons why you think vertebrates need a skeleton.

Things to do

1 Copy and complete:
All vertebrates belong to one of five main groups. The . . . . live in water all the time, breathe using . . . . and swim using . . . . The . . . . live part of their life on land but go to water to . . . . The . . . . have scaly skin and live all their life on land. . . . . are the only group of vertebrates that can fly. They have . . . . and . . . . to do this. . . . . have fur or . . . . and feed their young on . . . .

2 Which group do you think you belong to? Give your reasons.

3 Find out the names of 2 examples of each of the 5 main vertebrate groups that live wild in Britain.

4 A penguin and an osprey look very different. Write down 3 reasons why scientists think they belong to the same group.

5 In what ways do you think reptiles are better than amphibians at living on land?

It's a green world

What are plants? You already know that they are very different from animals. For one thing they make their own food.

For this reason, plants are often known as **producers** of food, whilst animals are **consumers** of food.

As with animals, you can put plants into groups to help you find their names.

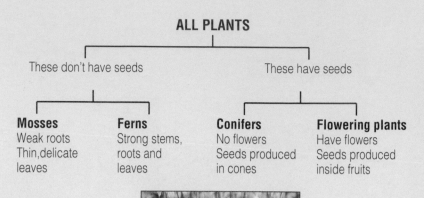

ALL PLANTS

These don't have seeds | These have seeds

Mosses
Weak roots
Thin,delicate
leaves

Ferns
Strong stems,
roots and
leaves

Conifers
No flowers
Seeds produced
in cones

Flowering plants
Have flowers
Seeds produced
inside fruits

Mosses

- Live in damp places
- Have thin leaves that easily lose water
- Make tiny **spores** instead of seeds. These are carried away by the wind. Moss spores grow into new moss plants.

▶ Look at the picture or at some moss plants.

a Where do you think the spores are made?

b How heavy do you think the spores will be? Give your reasons.

c Why do you think that mosses are only found in damp places?

Ferns

- Have strong stems, roots and leaves
- Make spores instead of seeds
- Have tubes that carry water around inside the plant. The tubes are called **xylem**.

▶ Look at a fern leaf.

d Where do you think the spores are made?

e How are they protected from the rain?

Conifers

- Many are evergreen with leaves like needles
- Have xylem tubes
- Their seeds are produced inside **cones**

▶ Look at a pine cone. Can you find the seeds inside it?

f How do you think these seeds are carried away?

Flowering plants

- Produce flowers
- Have xylem tubes
- Make **seeds** inside fruits and berries

▶ Try cutting open a broad bean seed or maize seed. ⚠
  Look for a **very young plant** and its **food store** surrounded
  by a **hard seed coat**.

g Write down your ideas about what each of these parts do.

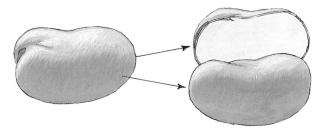

It's a fact!

The largest living plants are the giant redwoods of
North America that grow over 100 metres high.

Investigating water loss from leaves

Most flowering plants live on the land. Their leaves often lose water,
just as we lose water from our skin as sweat.

Plan an investigation to find out which sort of leaf is best at keeping
water. Choose 2 different types of leaf.

Remember that your tests must be fair.

How will you record your results?

Show your plan to your teacher.

Do your investigation and write your report.

1 Copy out and complete the following table.

Group	Do they have strong stems, roots and leaves?	Seeds or spores?	Flowers or not?
mosses ferns conifers flowering plants			

Things to do

2 Write down some examples of how
plants have become important as each of
the following:
a) food
b) fuel
c) medicine
d) building materials.

3 Over three million years ago, in what
was known as the Carboniferous age, vast
forests covered the Earth. The plants were
similar to the ones in this photograph. They
had stems, roots and leaves. These plants
reproduced by means of spores.
Which group of plants do they belong to?

Life's building blocks

What is a cell?

About 300 years ago Robert Hooke looked down his microscope at a thin layer of cork. He was able to see and draw what looked like tiny rooms. He called them '**cells**'.

With the help of a microscope you too will be able to see cells.

All living things are made up of cells. Some living things are made up of just one cell, but most are made up of many cells.

How big is a cell?

▶ Look at this photograph of human cheek cells. The cells are 1000 times larger than in real life.

Plan how you could work out the actual size of one of the cells in the photograph. Then work it out.

It's a fact

Your body probably contains about a million million cells!

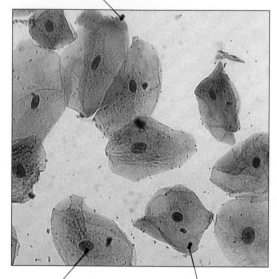

cell membrane: contains the cell and controls what passes in and out of the cell

nucleus: controls the cell and contains instructions to make more cells

cytoplasm: where the chemical reactions of the cell take place to keep the cell alive

Looking at plant cells

Make a slide of a thin piece of onion skin.

Look at it under the microscope at low power. What do you see?

Now look at the cells under the microscope at high magnification.

Your onion cells look different from the cheek cells shown above.

All plant cells have:

- a box-like shape
- a thick **cell wall** around the outside to support the cell
- a **vacuole** containing a watery solution called **cell sap**.

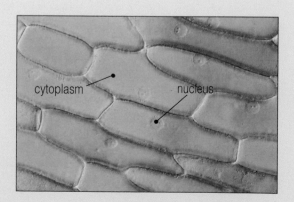

cytoplasm

nucleus

Looking at chloroplasts

Chloroplasts are very small structures that are found in many plant cells. They trap light energy during photosynthesis.

The energy helps plants to make their own food.

Why are there no chloroplasts in your onion cells?

Make a slide of a moss leaf.

Look at the cells under the microscope at high magnification. Can you see the chloroplasts?

Make a large drawing of 2 or 3 cells. Label the parts.

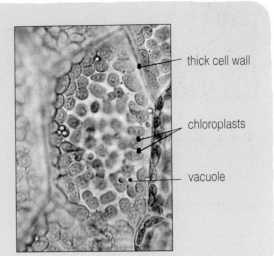

thick cell wall

chloroplasts

vacuole

Special cells

Lots of cells in plants and animals have changed their shape to do a particular job.

Look at these cells:

▶ In the table below the shapes of these cells and the jobs that they do are all jumbled up.

Copy out the table putting in the correct shape and job for each cell.

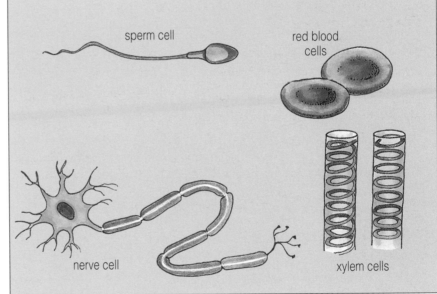

sperm cell

red blood cells

nerve cell

xylem cells

Type of cell	Shape	Job
sperm cell	hollow tube	carries oxygen
xylem cell	wire-like	swims to the egg
red blood cell	has a tail	carries water
nerve cell	flat disc	carries messages

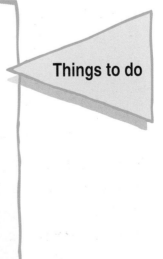

Things to do

1 Copy and complete this table.

	Cheek cell (animal)	Onion cell (plant)	Moss leaf cell (plant)
Does it have a nucleus?			
Does it have a cell wall?			
Does it have chloroplasts?			
Does it have a vacuole?			

2 Write down what you think each of the following cell parts do:
a) chloroplast
b) cell membrane
c) cell wall
d) nucleus.

3 Label the parts on the diagram of the microscope provided by your teacher.
Can you remember how you used the microscope?
Write down what each of the different parts is used for.

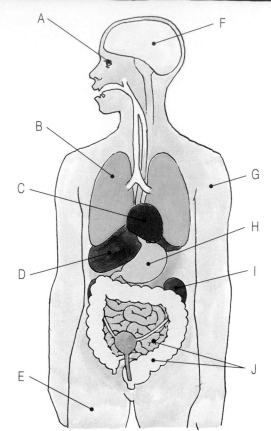

Getting ORGANised!

Do you know what **organs** are?

They are parts of your body that do a particular job for you,
e.g. your kidneys get rid of waste and control your water balance.

▶ Make a list of some other organs in your body and say what they do.

The see-through body

▶ Write down the letters A to J. Study the diagram opposite and
match each letter with one of the following parts of the body:

heart	eye	lungs	stomach	arm
liver	intestines	kidney	brain	leg

Different organs work together as part of a **system**, e.g. the stomach
and small intestine are part of the digestive system.

Organs are made up of **tissues**.
Tissues are made up of cells that are alike and do the same job.
The tissue in your muscles is made up of identical muscle cells.

Body construction kit

Cells:
The building blocks.

Muscle cells contract
and relax.

Tissue:
Similar cells working
together in the same way.

Muscle tissue is made of
muscle cells that contract
and relax together.

Organ:
Groups of tissues working
together.

Your heart is made up of
muscle tissue. It pumps
blood around your body.

System:
A group of organs working together.

Heart and blood vessels make up
your blood system. The blood system
carries blood around your body.

▶ Make a list of some types of cell found in your body and say what jobs they do.

It's a fact!

Most animals and plants have many different
types of cells all doing different jobs. Your body
has over 200 different types of cell!

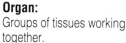

The working plant

Plants have bodies too. They are also made up of many different organs, such as leaves, flowers and roots.

▶ Write down the letters A to F. Study this diagram and match each letter with one of the following parts of the plant:

root	leaf	fruit	flower	bud	stem

Investigation: Beet this!

A beetroot is a plant organ that stores food over the winter. In the spring the new plant uses this food for growth. Beetroot tissue is made up of cells that contain a red dye. This dye leaks out if the cells are put into hot water.

How can you get the most dye out of a chip of beetroot?

Plan your investigation.

Decide what apparatus you will need and how you are going to record your results.

Remember that it must be a fair test.

Show your plan to your teacher and then start your investigation.

---

1 Copy and complete:
A tissue is made up of . . . . that carry out the same . . . . An organ is formed from groups of . . . . working together. A . . . . is a group of organs working together.

2 Copy out the organs listed on the left. Match each with the correct system from those listed on the right.

Lungs and windpipe	Blood system
Heart and vessels	Nervous system
Brain and spinal cord	Breathing system
Kidneys and bladder	Digestive system
Stomach and intestines	Excretory system

3 Imagine that you are a particular organ in the body. Write about what you are like and what job you do in the body. Don't forget to say why you think that you are so important.

4 Some parts of your body could be replaced if they wear out. Write down a list of artificial body parts and parts that you think could be transplanted.

Things to do

Questions

1 A visitor from outer space lands on Earth.
The first thing that it sees is a steam train passing by.
Give 2 reasons why the visitor thinks it is alive.
Give 2 reasons why you think the visitor is wrong.

2 Look at this photograph of an animal.
Do you think it is a vertebrate or
an invertebrate?
Which group do you think it belongs to?
Write down your reasons for your choice.

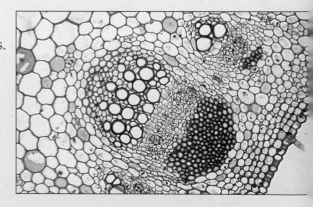

3 Cells can do different jobs.
Draw a cartoon character cell that does a particular job in the
human body.
Write about what your cell would do in a typical day.

4 Try putting some celery into coloured water. You can colour the
water with a little food colouring or ink. Leave your celery for a few
hours and then look at it. The coloured lines are xylem.
What job do you think xylem does?
Which plant groups have xylem and which do not?

5 Who am I?
a) I have 6 legs, and wings.
b) I have smooth, damp skin and spend part of my life in water.
c) I have a shell and move around on a muscular foot.
d) I have feathers and wings. I can fly!
e) I have 8 legs but no wings.

6 Look carefully at this photograph of plant cells.
How many different types of cell can you see?
Describe or draw each different cell.
Why don't they all look the same?

7 When using your microscope, why should you:
a) never touch the surfaces of the lenses or mirror?
b) put a cover slip over what you want to observe on a slide?
c) focus on low power first before turning up to high power?

Forces

5

Your life is full of forces.

Everything that you do needs a force.
To lift up your pen needs a force.
To turn the page needs a force.

In the photo, the people are being pulled down the slide by the force of gravity. And they are being slowed by another force – the force of friction.

In this topic you can investigate forces, to find out what they can do and how to measure them.

Using forces

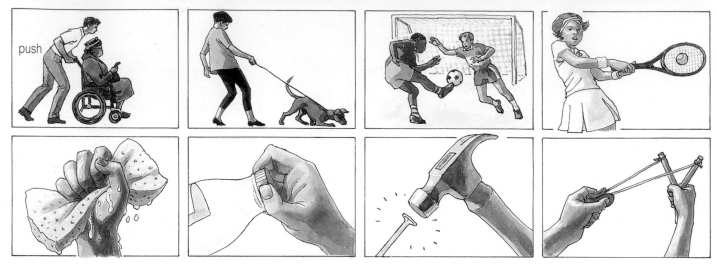

All these people are using **forces**.

▶ Look at the pictures above and find the force in each one.

a Write down a list of words that describe the forces in the pictures. Your first word can be **_push_**.

b Write down 5 things that you have done today using a force. Which muscles did you use**?**

Force-meters

▶ Look at diagrams 1 to 4, of some **force-meters**: They are sometimes called newton-meters or spring-balances.

Each one is measuring the size of a force. We measure the size of a force in **newtons** (also written as **N**).

c For each force-meter, write down the largest force that it can measure on its scale.

d What force is each one showing on its scale here**?**

e The apple is pulling down with a force called its **weight**. What is the weight of the apple**?**

The weight of this book is about 5 newtons.

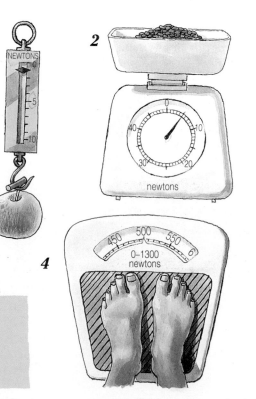

It's a fact! An ant can pull with a force of $\frac{1}{1000}$ newton, a family car can push with 5000 newtons, and a moon-rocket exerts 30 million N.

Measuring forces

This table lists some jobs that need a force:

Copy out the table.

In each case, first make a **prediction** of how big you think the force will be. Write it down.

Then **measure** that force with a force-meter.
Take care to choose the right force-meter for each job.

	Size of force in newtons	
	Prediction	Actual
Lift a bag	20 ?	
Pull a stool along the floor		
Pull the stool more quickly		
Weigh a Bunsen burner		
Stretch a rubber-band to twice its length		
Open a door		

Finger strength

Plan an investigation to find the strength of people's finger muscles.

You can use bathroom scales as shown, and test several different people.

- How will you ensure it is a fair test?
- How will you record your results?
- How can you make your results more reliable?

Ask your teacher to check your plan, and then do your investigation.

Is there any pattern in your results?

1 Copy and complete:
Forces can do 3 things. They can:
a) change the **size** or **shape** of an object (for example: squeezing a sponge)
b) change the speed of an object to make it move **faster** (for example: kicking a ball) or to make it move . . . . (for example: catching a ball)
c) change the **direction** of a moving object (e.g. a ball bouncing off a . . . .).

2 Sketch 3 of the pictures at the top of the opposite page and mark with an arrow where you think a force is acting.
For example:

3 Suppose you are given a ruler, a rubber-band, a paper-clip, some cotton thread and some sellotape. How could you use these to make your own force-meter?
Draw a diagram of your design and label it.

4 The newton is named after Sir Isaac Newton, a famous scientist who lived 300 years ago.

Do some research, and then write 2 paragraphs about him.

Things to do

A small push can slide this book along the table. But why does it stop moving**?**

The book is touching the table, and they are both rough. When they rub together, the force of **friction** slows down the book.

Friction can be useful.

You can't walk unless there is friction between your shoes and the ground.

▶ List 3 other examples where friction is helpful to us.

Friction can be a problem.

If there is too much friction in a bicycle, then it is hard to pedal.

Because of friction some of your energy is used to warm up the moving parts. This is like rubbing your hands together to make them warm (see page 34).

You can make the friction less by **lubricating** the moving parts with oil or grease.

▶ Look at this photo of a bicycle:
Copy the table and fill in as many examples in each column as you can.

Friction is a **contact** force. It only happens if things are touching.

Other forces can act at a distance, without touching. Here are 3 examples:

The surface of paper is rough (magnified x100)

Riding a bicycle	
Friction is needed	Friction is not wanted
tyres on the road	

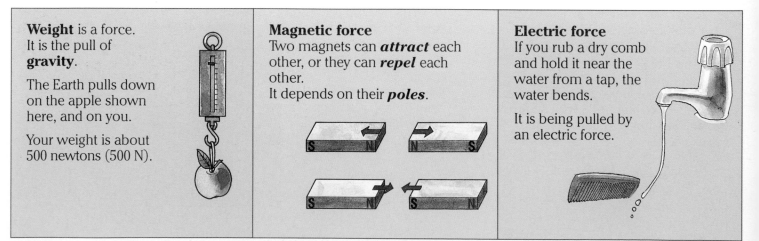

Weight is a force. It is the pull of **gravity**.

The Earth pulls down on the apple shown here, and on you.

Your weight is about 500 newtons (500 N).

Magnetic force
Two magnets can **attract** each other, or they can **repel** each other.
It depends on their **poles**.

Electric force
If you rub a dry comb and hold it near the water from a tap, the water bends.

It is being pulled by an electric force.

Investigating shoes

Imagine you are a shoe designer.
You have been asked to design some shoes that have a good 'grip' so that they won't slide easily.

Here are some things that make a shoe slide easily or not:

a the type of sole
b the ground surface it is on
c the weight of the person in the shoe.

Choose **one** of these (**a**, **b** or **c**).

Then find out how changing it makes the shoe more or less easy to slide.

- What do you need to change and what do you need to measure?

- How will you ensure it is a fair test? What things (variables) do you need to keep the same each time?

- How will you record your results?

Ask your teacher to check your plan, and then do it.

What pattern do you find?

Air resistance (or ***drag***) can be a problem.
Cars are ***streamlined*** to reduce air friction.

▶ How does the shape of dolphins help them?

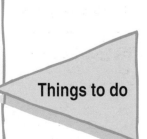

---

1 Copy and complete:
a) Friction is a . . . . which tries to slow down objects when they rub together.
b) Friction can be reduced by . . . . the moving parts with oil. Air resistance can be reduced by . . . . the shape of a car.
c) Weight is a . . . . It is the pull of . . . . by the Earth.
d) Two other forces are magnetic . . . . and electric . . . .

2 Suppose you wake up tomorrow morning and find that there is no friction at all in your home.
Write 2 paragraphs to describe what could happen to you.

3 How can you reduce the friction in a bicycle?

4 Why is friction important for road safety? What can happen if the weather is
a) wet? b) icy?

5 Make a table as shown:

Friction is needed	Friction is not wanted
catching a ball	swimming

Think about different sports, and list 5 examples in each column.

Things to do

5c Floating and sinking

You know that some things **float** on water and some things **sink**.

The diagram shows some 'floaters' and some 'sinkers'.

Floating in the salty water of the Dead Sea in Israel

▶ Draw up a table with 2 columns labelled 'floaters' and 'sinkers'. Fill in your table from the diagram.

▶ Which column do you think each of these would go in:
  • stone?
  • paper?
  • soap?

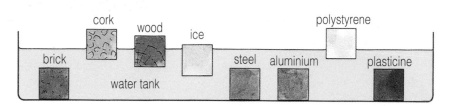

Why do things float or sink?

Hang a 'sinker' from a force-meter (spring-balance).

Write down the reading on the force-meter. This is the **weight** of the object. It is the pull of gravity by the Earth.

Push up your finger under the object. What happens to the force-meter reading?

Now gently lower the object into a beaker of water. What happens to the reading on the force-meter?

Copy the table and fill in the first line.

Repeat the experiment with a 'floater'. What do you find?

Try some more 'floaters' and 'sinkers'.

Can you see a rule which is true for all the things that float?

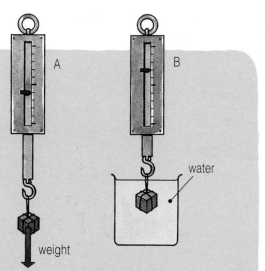

Name of object	Does it float or sink?	Weight in air (newtons)	Weight in water (newtons)	∴ Change in weight (newtons)
1.				
2.				

When an object is lowered into the water, the water pushes up on it. This force is called an **upthrust**.

If the object floats, the upthrust is equal to the weight. The two forces balance out. They are **balanced forces**.

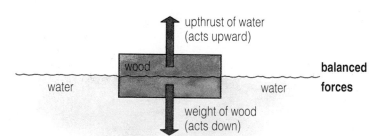

upthrust of water (acts upward)

wood

water   water   **balanced forces**

weight of wood (acts down)

64

Boats and balloons

A boat floats on water because of the upthrust.

If the boat weighs 10 000 newtons then the water must give an upthrust of 10 000 newtons.

A boat will float higher or lower depending on the **density** of the water.

Salty sea-water is *more dense* than fresh-water, so a boat floats higher in the salty sea than in a fresh-water lake.

A hydrogen balloon can float in air because the air gives it a small upthrust.

Investigating boats

Design and build a boat that will support as much weight as possible.

You can use:
either 50 grams of plasticine (this weighs half a newton = 0.5 N)
or   a piece of kitchen foil of size 10 cm × 10 cm.

Your boat should: • float
• be stable (not fall over)
• carry a cargo.

For cargo you can use coins, paper-clips, marbles or small weights.

Try out different designs. Sketch them to keep a record.

A challenge! Whose boat can carry the heaviest cargo?

---

1 Copy and complete:
a) Weight is a . . . . caused by the pull of . . . .
b) An object placed in water has a force called . . . . pushing up on it.
c) When an object floats, the upthrust is . . . . to the weight of the object. The two forces are . . . .

2 A steel block sinks in water. A steel ship floats. Try to explain why they are different.

3 Ships have marks on their sides called **Plimsoll lines**. They show the levels at which the ship should float in different waters.

Look at this diagram.

Which mark (A or B) do you think is for:
a) fresh-water in a lake?
b) sea-water?

Things to do

Forces at work

Levers

A lever is a simple **machine**. It helps us to do jobs more easily.

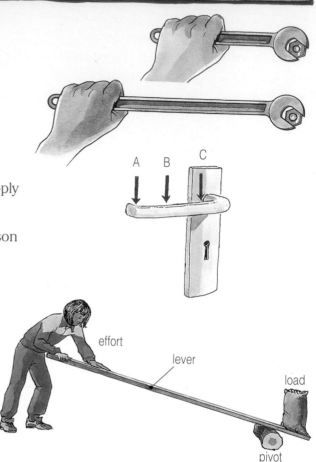

▶ The diagram shows two spanners, used for turning a nut on a bolt.

Which spanner would you use to undo a very tight nut? How can you make it even easier to undo the nut?

▶ Look at the door handle in the diagram:
It is a lever. Which is the best place (A, B or C) for you to apply a force? (Try this if you can.)

▶ Design a simple machine or tool that would help an old person to turn a stiff door handle. Draw a diagram and label it.

Here is a lever being used to lift a **load** (the sack):
The pivot (or '**fulcrum**') is near the sack.
The girl is applying an **effort** force to turn the lever and lift the load.
In this case, a small effort force can lift a large load.
This lever is a **force-magnifier**.

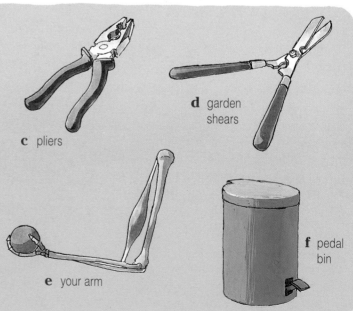

effort

lever

load

pivot

Sometimes levers are used as **distance-magnifiers**.
The long hand on a clock is a distance magnifier; a small movement near the centre of the clock becomes a big movement at the end of the pointer.
There are levers in your body that are used like this.
Bend your arm and think about what is happening.

Here are some common machines using levers.
For each one, write down:
- where the pivot is
- where the effort force is applied (by you)
- where the load is
- whether it is a force-magnifier or a distance-magnifier.

a wheelbarrow

b opening a paint tin

c pliers

d garden shears

e your arm

f pedal bin

Pulleys

A **pulley** is another simple machine.

Here are two pulley systems that could be used on a building site:

What are pulley systems useful for?

Investigate these two pulley systems.

You can use a clamp stand to hold up the top pulley. You can use slotted weights for the load. You can measure the effort force with a force-meter (spring-balance).

Measure the effort needed to lift up different loads.

What do you find?

Which pulley system is easier to use?

Ring a bell

The diagram shows a design for a door-bell in an old castle.

When the handle is pulled:

g What happens to the blue rope?

h Which way does pulley A turn?

i Which way does lever B move?

j Which way does the red rope move?

k What happens to the bell?

l Is lever C a force-magnifier or a distance-magnifier?

m Can you design a simpler system? Draw a diagram of it.

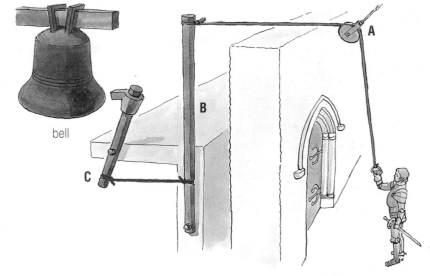

bell

1 Copy and complete:
a) Levers and pulleys are simple . . . .
b) A lever has a pivot or . . . .
c) A lever can be a . . . . -magnifier or a . . . . -magnifier.

2 Think about the ways you can move your arms, fingers, legs, jaw, etc.
Make a list of the levers in your body.
For 3 of these levers, draw a simple diagram and show where the pivot is.

3 Design a handle for a bathroom tap to be used by an old person or invalid.

4 Imagine you are using a spanner to undo a tight nut. Copy and complete this Energy Transfer Diagram (see page 34):

. . . . stored in my body → . . . . energy of the nut as it turns

. . . . warming up the nut (due to friction)

5 Design a system of pulleys and levers that will allow you to open the front door of your house from your bedroom.
Sketch a diagram of your system.

Move it!

To move something you have to apply a **force**. You looked at this in lesson 5a (see page 61).

a push force is needed to start moving

▶ Look at the cartoon:

a Which one needs the bigger force to start moving – the heavy man or the little girl?

Now suppose both sledges are moving across the ice, at the same speed.

b Which one needs a bigger force to stop it?

Objects usually slow down and stop, because of friction (see page 62).

c What happens to the sledge if there is very little friction?

d What do you think would happen to it if there was no friction at all?

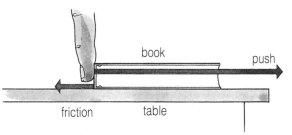

We show forces in diagrams by arrows.
The bigger the force, the longer the arrow.

▶ Look at the diagram. It shows a book being pushed across a table.

e Which is the bigger force: the push of the finger or the force of friction?

f Do you think the book is moving? Why?

g How big is the push force in newtons? (Use your ruler to measure it.)

h How big is the friction force?

scale: 1 cm stands for 1 newton

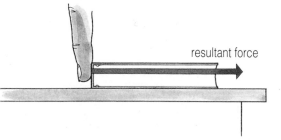

The friction force cancels out part of the push force. We are left with a **resultant** force.

i How big is the resultant force here?

j What would be the resultant force if the push force = 3 newtons and the friction force = 2 newtons?

It is the resultant force that makes the book move.
The bigger the resultant force, the faster the book moves.

▶ Draw a diagram of the book and show a push force of 2 newtons and a friction force of 2 newtons.

k What is the resultant force?

l Does the book move or stay still?

Isaac Newton wrote a 'law' about these ideas:

If an object has **no** resultant force on it, then

• if it is at rest, it stays at rest (not moving)

• if it is moving, it keeps moving at a steady speed in a straight line.

Investigating movement

Let a toy car roll down a slope:

Plan an investigation to see how the **time taken** by a car to travel down depends on the **height** it starts from.

You can use a pair of *light gates*: As the car passes through the first gate it starts an electrical timer. The timer stops as the car passes the second gate. The computer shows how long it took.

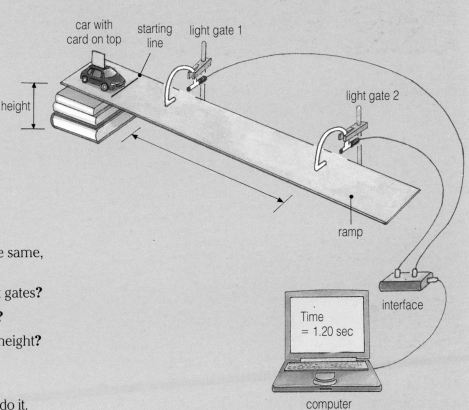

car with card on top · starting line · light gate 1 · light gate 2 · height · ramp · interface · Time = 1.20 sec · computer

What do you think will happen? Write down your **prediction**.

- Make a list of things you will keep the same, to make it a fair test.
- How far apart will you place the light gates?
- Will you push the car or just let it go?
- How often will you repeat it at each height?
- How will you record your results?

Show your plan to your teacher and then do it.

What did you find out? Does it agree with your prediction?

Now answer these questions. In your answers, try to include some of the words in the box.

weight	pull of gravity
resultant force	friction
potential energy	kinetic energy

m Why does the car move down the ramp?

n What is the name given to the energy that the car has at the top?

o Where did this energy come from?

p What is the name given to the energy it has at the bottom?

q Where is the energy when the car has stopped?

---

1 Copy and complete:
a) An object can have . . . . than one force acting on it.
b) If there is no resultant . . . . on the object, its movement does . . . . change.
c) Newton's law on this says:
if an object has no . . . . force on it, then
  - if it is at rest then it stays at . . . . (not . . . .)
  - if it is moving then it keeps on . . . . at a . . . . speed in a . . . . line.

2 Use a scale of 1 cm for 1 newton to draw force diagrams for:
a) a book being pushed by a force of 6 N with a friction force of 2 N
b) a toy boat weighing 4 N floating on water (see the diagram on page 64).

3 Look at the next page and collect a suitable bottle or can, to bring to the next lesson.

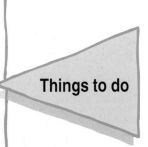

Things to do

Rubber-band racers

▶ Look at these diagrams of some rubber-band racers.
Choose **one** of them and then build it.

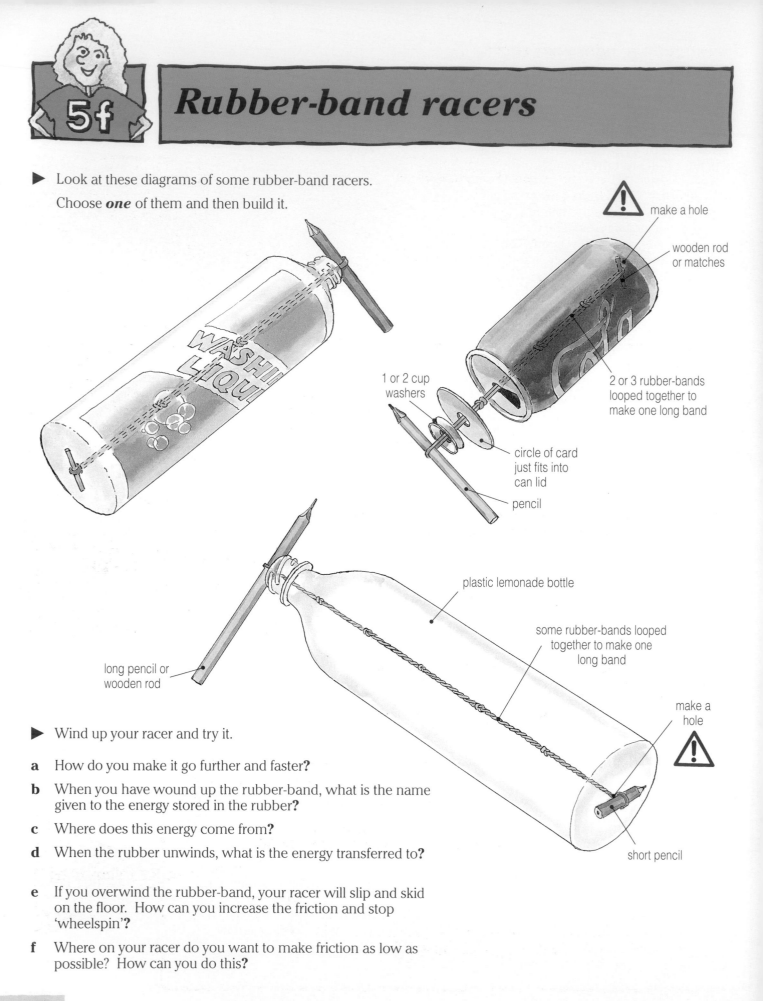

make a hole

wooden rod
or matches

2 or 3 rubber-bands
looped together to
make one long band

circle of card
just fits into
can lid

pencil

1 or 2 cup
washers

plastic lemonade bottle

some rubber-bands looped
together to make one
long band

long pencil or
wooden rod

make a
hole

short pencil

▶ Wind up your racer and try it.

a How do you make it go further and faster?

b When you have wound up the rubber-band, what is the name
given to the energy stored in the rubber?

c Where does this energy come from?

d When the rubber unwinds, what is the energy transferred to?

e If you overwind the rubber-band, your racer will slip and skid
on the floor. How can you increase the friction and stop
'wheelspin'?

f Where on your racer do you want to make friction as low as
possible? How can you do this?

Investigations with your racer

▶ Choose **one** of these investigations.

Plan it carefully (see page 18).
Make sure it is a fair test.
When your plan is complete, do the investigation.

1 Investigate how to make your racer travel in a straight line.

Whose racer can travel a straight 3 metre course in the shortest time**?**

2 Investigate how your racer travels up a hill. How steep can you make the slope?

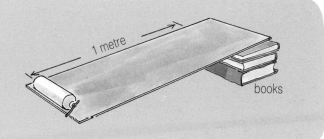

1 metre

books

Whose racer can travel for 1 metre up the steepest slope**?**

3 Investigate how the speed of your racer depends on the number of turns that you wind it up.

$$\text{average speed} = \frac{\text{distance travelled}}{\text{time taken}}$$

You will need a stop-clock.
You can use the formula shown in the box.

▶ Make a report on what you did and what you found out. It can be a written report or a poster.

▶ If you have time, you can do another one of these investigations.

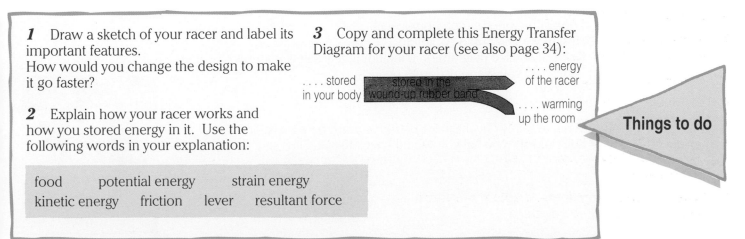

1 Draw a sketch of your racer and label its important features.
How would you change the design to make it go faster?

2 Explain how your racer works and how you stored energy in it. Use the following words in your explanation:

food   potential energy   strain energy
kinetic energy   friction   lever   resultant force

3 Copy and complete this Energy Transfer Diagram for your racer (see also page 34):

. . . . stored in your body → . . . stored in the wound-up rubber band → . . . . energy of the racer / . . . . warming up the room

Things to do

71

Questions

A kingfisher diving into water

1 Streamlining reduces friction.
Give 3 examples of streamlining in animals, and explain how it helps the animals.

2 How is friction reduced in:
a) a hovercraft?
b) a racing car?
c) a yacht?

3 The table tells you about the braking distances for a car going at 15 metres per second (33 m.p.h.):

Braking distances		
Dry road	new tyres	13 metres
	old tyres	14 metres
Wet road	new tyres	18 metres
	old tyres	23 metres

a) Draw a bar-chart of the data, and label it.
b) What is the best combination of road and tyres for stopping quickly? What is the braking distance in this case?
c) What is the worst combination? How much worse is it than the best combination?
d) Why is it harder to stop on wet roads than on dry roads?

4 Plan an investigation to compare the brakes on different bicycles.
How would you make it a **fair** test?
How would you make it a **safe** test?
What measurements would you make?
(Do not do this investigation without adult supervision.)

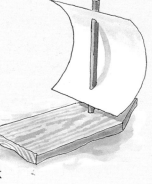

5 Plan an investigation of a toy sailing boat.
Decide what you would investigate, and how you would make it a fair test.
What features would a good design have?

6 Design a machine to help someone who can't bend their back to pick up a book from the floor.

7 Look at the photograph on page 59.
Design your own slide or chute.
Draw a labelled diagram of it, including any safety features.
Where do you want friction to be:
a) low?   b) high?

8 Write a 'safety checklist' for **either** a pram **or** a bicycle.
It should show what you would check to see if it is safe to use.

Acids and alkalis

6

Have you heard of acids and alkalis?
What do you know about them already?

These substances are important to us in everyday life. They are used to make clothes, paints, soaps, fertilisers, medicines and many other things.

There are even acids and alkalis inside your body!
Your stomach wall makes acid. If too much acid is made, it can be a problem. In this topic you can find out how to solve the problem.

You might also think about the 'hydrangea plant mystery'. How can you make the plant grow blue flowers this year ... and pink flowers next year?

A question of acid or alkali

▶ Write down 5 words that come to mind when you hear the word **acid**.

▶ What do you think an acid is?
You could use some of your 5 words to help you write a sentence.
I think an acid is …

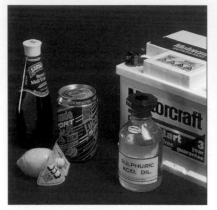

All these contain acids

All these contain alkalis

▶ Think of as many examples as you can of opposites, e.g. big/small.

Acids and **alkalis** are *chemical* opposites.

Indicators can be used to show which things are acids and which things are alkalis.

Have you ever used **litmus** indicator? Litmus is a useful indicator. It can be in the form of a paper or a liquid. It is a purple dye which turns *red* in acid and *blue* in alkali.

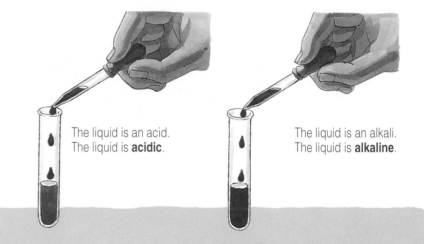

The liquid is an acid.
The liquid is **acidic**.

The liquid is an alkali.
The liquid is **alkaline**.

Making your own indicators

Some brightly coloured berries, flower petals and vegetables make good indicators.

Look at the pictures to see how you can make your own indicator.

Crush your plant pieces.

Add a little methylated spirit.

Keep crushing until all the colour has come out.

Use a pipette to put the liquid into a test-tube.

You can use this method to make some indicators for the next investigation.

Which indicator is the best?

In your group discuss what makes a good indicator.

Make a list of your ideas.

Use these ideas to find out which of the petals, fruits or berries makes the best indicator. Remember you will need to do fair tests.

How can you make your results reliable?

Use the method shown on the opposite page to make your own indicators.

When you have made your indicators your teacher can give you some acids and alkalis for your tests.

Write a report on what you did.

Which was the best indicator?

How could you improve your investigation?

Which indicator is the best?
Prediction
Plan
Results
Conclusion
Our best indicator
was:
because:
Evaluation

It's a fact!

Drivers who transport acids and alkalis must carry **Tremcards**. This stands for Transport Emergency Cards. The cards tell the driver what to do if there is an emergency.

---

1 Copy the sentences below into your book filling in the blanks.
Acids are the chemical opposites of . . . .
Indicators are one . . . . in acids and another . . . . in alkalis.
Litmus is a useful indicator. It turns red in . . . . and blue in . . . .

2 What do all the alkalis in the picture at the top of the opposite page have in common?

3 On the Tremcard for dilute hydrochloric acid the emergency action for a spillage is:

> • Drench with water
> • If the substance has entered a sewer advise police

Why do you think it says this on the Tremcard?

4 Name these pieces of apparatus.

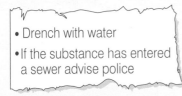
a) b) c) d) e)

What are a) and b) used for?

5 Write explanations for the following:
a) bottles of hydrochloric acid have warning labels
b) bottles of lemon juice do not have warning labels
c) acids are usually kept in glass bottles, not in metal containers.

6 Think about the practical work you did in today's lesson. Make a list of things you did well. Make a list of things you didn't do well. Write down 2 things you could improve next time.

Things to do

How strong?

► Crack the code to find out what you will be asked to do today!

Take:

- The second letter of the word: A rainbow has 7 of these.
- The first letter of the word: The colour of an alkali with litmus.
- The first letter of the word: You wash your hands with this.
- The second letter of the word: An acid you put on pancakes.
- The last letter of the word: It detects acids and alkalis.
- The first letter of the word: An acid served on chips.
- The second letter of the word: The colour of an acid with litmus.

You can use indicators to test for acids and alkalis.

Universal indicator is a mixture of a few indicators. It is very useful because it tells you how ***strong*** or how ***weak*** the acids and alkalis are. You can get universal indicator as a liquid or as paper.

Testing acids and alkalis

Your teacher will give you some solutions to test.

Put one of the solutions in a test-tube (about a quarter full).

Add a few drops of universal indicator. Shake this tube carefully. What do you see?

Use the colour chart to find the **pH number** of your solution.

⚠ acids alkalis

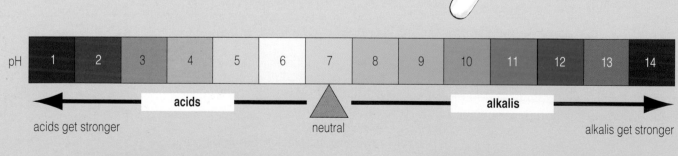

Test the other solutions with universal indicator.

Write down the ***colour*** and ***pH number*** each time. Record whether the solution is an acid or an alkali.

Which is the strongest acid?
Which is the strongest alkali?

Substance	Colour	pH	Acid or alkali?

Acid rain

Have you heard about the **acid rain** problem? When fuels burn they make gases which move into the air. These gases are made of acids – they are acidic. The gases dissolve in water in the clouds. When it rains the acids are brought back to earth. Acid rain can damage buildings and trees. It affects our **environment**.

Stonework damaged by acid rain

The effect acid rain can have on trees

Carry out this investigation to see how acid rain affects stonework.

Add a few drops of acid to some crushed limestone.
Write down what you see.

What do you think would happen if you used a weaker acid?
Write down what you expect to see.

Now try it with the weaker acid.

Was your prediction correct?

Do you think acid rain is a strong or weak acid? Why?

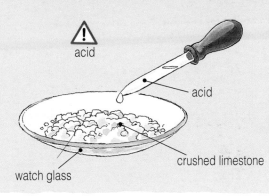

1 Match each of these pH numbers with the correct statement.

pH6	strong acid
pH1	strong alkali
pH14	weak acid
pH8	weak alkali

2 Copy and complete this sentence.
Universal indicator is more useful than litmus because …

3 Answer the following questions about acid rain.
a) Look at the photograph at the top of this page and describe what acid rain does to trees.
b) Write down 3 ways in which humans could make less acid rain.
c) Look at your answer to b). Draw a poster to get the message across.

4 Kate says "I think milk gets more acidic if it is left out of the fridge for a long time." Do you think she is right? Plan an investigation to test Kate's idea.

5 How could you use the crushed limestone and acid test to put 4 acids in order of their strength?

Things to do

6c A balancing act

▶ Look back to the pH chart on page 76. Find the pH number of a solution which is neither acidic nor alkaline.

a What colour is universal indicator in this solution?

I think it's an acid.

Solutions which are neither acids nor alkalis are **neutral**.

You can make neutral solutions by mixing acids and alkalis together. The acid and alkali can balance each other out.

ACID + ALKALI → NEUTRAL SOLUTION

I think it's an alkali.

▶ Copy the diagrams below into your book. The 3 labels are missing. Choose the correct labels from the list to complete your diagrams.

- water
- acid
- acid and indicator
- alkali
- neutral solution and indicator
- indicator
- neutral solution
- alkali and indicator

Neutralising your stomach!

Did you know that there is acid in your stomach?

Have you ever had a stomach ache? Sometimes this can be caused by your stomach making too much acid.

Indigestion tablets or stomach powders can be used to 'settle' your stomach.

Do you think these tablets and powders are acids, alkalis or neutral? Why?

▶ Have you seen any advertisements about curing indigestion?

Write down the names of some cures.

SCI-CO HEALTHCARE

Your health is our care

MEMO TO: *Analysts*   FROM: *Chris Williams*

The company wishes to test three stomach powders, A, B and C, to see how well they neutralise stomach acid.

Please carry out some tests to tell me how much of each powder you need to neutralise the stomach acid. Make sure you do fair tests. Be as accurate as possible.

Our first tests show that one powder will not work at all. Please check this. I'd like a report on:

(a) how you carried out the tests - including all measurements you made

(b) your results

(c) which powder is best at neutralising stomach acid.

This is urgent! Thanks.

It's a fact!

The bacteria in your mouth can change sugary food into acid. If the acid stays in your mouth for a long time, it attacks your teeth. This causes tooth decay. Toothpastes often contain weak alkali to neutralise acid in the mouth.

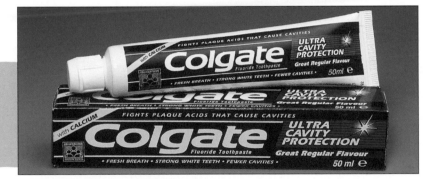

Things to do

1 Copy and complete:
A substance with a . . . . number of 4 is an . . . . If a weak . . . . is added to it, the solution can become neutral with a pH number of . . . .

2 Acid can cause tooth decay! Design and make a leaflet to tell young children about the need to brush teeth regularly.

3 In the last few lessons you have been using different indicators – litmus, universal indicator, and some you made yourself from petals, berries or vegetables.
Why is universal indicator the best one to use when neutralising acids or alkalis?

4 Find out about some medicines used to treat stomach acid and indigestion.
a) Make a list of their ingredients.
b) Are there any chemicals in common? If so, give their names.
c) List the names of the medicines in a table like this.

Tablet	Powder	Liquid

d) Medicines can be sold as tablets, powder or liquid.
Write down an advantage of each of these.
e) What other things would you consider before choosing a medicine to cure indigestion?

pH is pretty Helpful

pH in the garden

The pH of a soil is very important. Some plants grow well in acidic soil. Some would grow better in neutral or alkaline soil.

Gardeners and farmers need to know the pH of their soil. The soil gets too acidic sometimes. This can stop plants growing well. The farmers could add lime (an alkali) to change the pH of the soil.

It's a fact!

You can buy pH test kits from garden centres to test your own soil.

Testing soils

Your teacher will give you some different soils to test.

Take your first soil sample and put 2 spatula measures in a test-tube. Add about 5 cm³ of distilled water. Stopper the tube and shake it for about a minute.

Set up a filter funnel and paper. Filter the soil mixture into another test-tube. Add universal indicator to the filtrate. Record the pH value.

Repeat this test with other soils.

soil and distilled water — filter paper — filter funnel — soil — filtrate

Soil sample	pH value
A	
B	
.	
.	
.	

Write down answers to the following questions.

a Why do you use **distilled** water in this test?

b Why do you 'shake for about a minute'?

c Which soil is the most acidic?

d Which soil is the most alkaline?

Look at the plant pH preference list (opposite) from the pH test kit.

e Which of your soil samples do you think could grow
(i) apples (ii) potatoes (iii) blackcurrants?

f Which crops could soil A grow?

Plant pH preference	
Name	pH preference
apple	5.0–6.5
potato	4.5–6.0
blackcurrant	6.0–8.0
mint	7.0–8.0
onion	6.0–7.0
strawberry	5.0–7.0
lettuce	6.0–7.0

pH all around you

▶ In your group discuss the following pictures.

- Decide whether you all agree with the statements.
- Choose one statement to test. What would you do?
- If there is time, your teacher may let you try this.

You can use lemon juice to remove 'scale' from a kettle.

If we measure the pH of rainwater, it can tell us about air pollution.

acid

Vinegar is an acid. It should carry a hazard warning.

All shampoos are pH balanced.

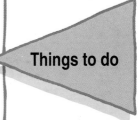

Acid drop sweets are not really acids.

---

1 Make a drawing to show which plant would grow best in each pot.

2 Lime has a pH value of about 9. Citric acid has a pH value of about 4. Which should you add to a neutral soil to grow apples?

3 Acids and alkalis can be dangerous substances.
You must be careful when you use them. Design a warning poster for your laboratory.

4 Plan an investigation to see how the pH of soil depends on the amount of lime added to it.

5 Fertilisers are used to help plants grow. They give nutrients (food) to the soil and can change its pH value.
Do you think we should use fertilisers? Why? Why not?

Things to do

Questions

1 Design and make a poster to explain the word **acid**.
Use key words and clear drawings.

2 Indicators can be made by crushing some plants and vegetables with a liquid. You can use propanone or methylated spirit to make an indicator with red cabbage.
Jill says that proponane is better at removing the colour.
Plan an investigation to see if she is right.

3 Write a report on the different uses of acids in the home.

4 Make a list of all the chemical indicators you have used in this topic.
Which indicator was the most useful? Why?

5 Read the letter to a newspaper shown here. Write a reply to Mr. Clark. Say whether you agree or disagree with his ideas.

I'm fed up with all these chemical tankers on our roads. Many of them carry dangerous things such as acids. Any spills from the tankers could kill people. I think tankers should only be allowed to use the roads between 11 pm and 6 am. Then there are fewer cars around. I want the government to make this law. Will others support me?
Mr. C. Clark

6 A local farmer wants to neutralise his acidic soil. He cannot decide whether to use CALCOLIME or SUPERCAL for this.
a) Plan an investigation to find out which is better at neutralising the soil.
b) What other factors should the farmer consider before choosing which to use?

7 If you leave a half-eaten apple in the air it goes brown.
Keeping pieces of apple in a solution of lemon juice slows down the rate of browning.
Do you think this could be something to do with the pH of the solution?
Make a prediction.
Plan an investigation to test your prediction.

Growing up

7

As we grow up, each of us changes from a baby to a child, then to a teenager and eventually to an adult.

But growing up doesn't just mean we get bigger. We also grow up in other ways.

We develop mentally. Our emotions change as we mix with other people. Most of us will find a partner and may have children of our own. Then we will have responsibilities to our partner and to our children.

Having babies

▶ Look at the different stages in a human life shown here:

Put them in the correct order starting with the youngest.

Baby talk

Why do people decide to have a baby? Some of the reasons that people give for having children are shown below.

▶ Discuss in groups which you think are good reasons and which are not. Try to put the reasons in order starting with the one you agree with most.

> People would think that there was something wrong if we didn't have children.

> I want a son to take to football matches.

> Bringing up children will be a challenge.

> We just love children.

> Having children will bring us closer together.

> We want to enjoy bringing up a family.

> Children will bring more money into the house.

> Our children will look after us when we are old.

> Our parents would love to have grandchildren.

▶ When do you think is the best time for a couple to have a baby?

When do you think is the wrong time?

What sort of preparations do you think will have to be made before the baby is born?

How are babies made?

To start a baby the male and female sex cells must join together. A **sperm** from a man must join with an **egg** from a woman. This is called **fertilisation**. In humans it occurs inside the woman's body.

Here are the parts of a man that are used for making sperms:

▶ Your teacher will give you a copy of this diagram.

a Shade in blue where sperms are made.

b Shade in red where fluid is added to the sperms.

c Shade in yellow the tubes that the sperms pass through to get to the outside.

d List the parts that the sperms pass through.

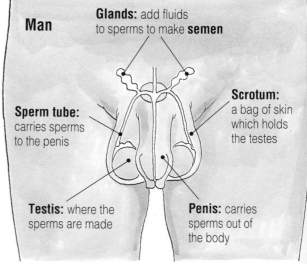

Man

Glands: add fluids to sperms to make **semen**

Sperm tube: carries sperms to the penis

Scrotum: a bag of skin which holds the testes

Testis: where the sperms are made

Penis: carries sperms out of the body

84

Here are the parts of a woman that are used to make eggs and produce babies:

▶ Your teacher will give you a copy of this diagram.

e Shade in blue where eggs are made.

f Shade in red where fertilisation may take place.

g Shade in yellow where the baby develops.

h List the parts that the egg would pass through on its way out of the body.

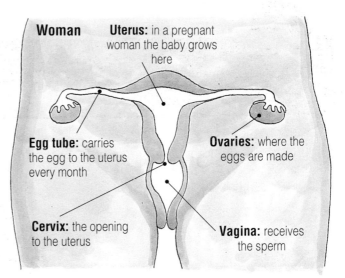

Woman

Uterus: in a pregnant woman the baby grows here

Egg tube: carries the egg to the uterus every month

Ovaries: where the eggs are made

Cervix: the opening to the uterus

Vagina: receives the sperm

It's a fact!

When a girl is born she has thousands of partly-formed eggs in each ovary. When she grows into a woman an egg will be released from one of her ovaries about every 28 days.

▶ Copy out these sentences and add as much as you can, using words from the box opposite:
- I know that females have …
- I know that males have …
- Fertilisation is when …
- Babies grow …

Now make some sentences of your own using some of these words.

| testes | egg | uterus | sperms |
| vagina | egg tube | sperm tube |

where eggs are made

| penis | ovaries | scrotum |

where sperms are made

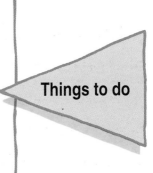

Things to do

1 Copy out the words in the following list. If you think that they are female put (F) after them. If you think that they are male put (M).

ovaries	egg tube	penis
uterus	testes	vagina
scrotum	sperm tube	cervix

2 Sometimes a woman's egg tubes get blocked.
a) Why do you think that a woman with both egg tubes blocked cannot have a baby?
b) Why do you think that a woman with one egg tube blocked might be able to have a baby?

3 Copy out the list of organs on the left and match each organ with its correct job from the list on the right.

penis	carries sperms to penis
ovaries	where the baby grows
sperm tube	makes sperms
vagina	carries eggs to uterus
uterus	makes eggs
testes	receives sperms
egg tube	holds testes
scrotum	carries sperms out of body

Fertilisation

▶ Look at these photographs of the human sperm and the human egg. Write down as many differences as you can between the sperm and the egg.

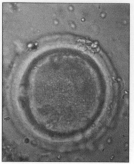
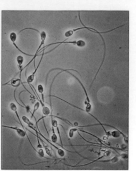

Human egg   Human sperm

Making love

When people 'make love' or 'have sex' it is not just so that they can have babies. Men and women can enjoy making love at other times too. They use it as a way of showing their love for each other. By having sex a man and women can feel very close to each other. Making love is far more than putting a sperm and an egg together.

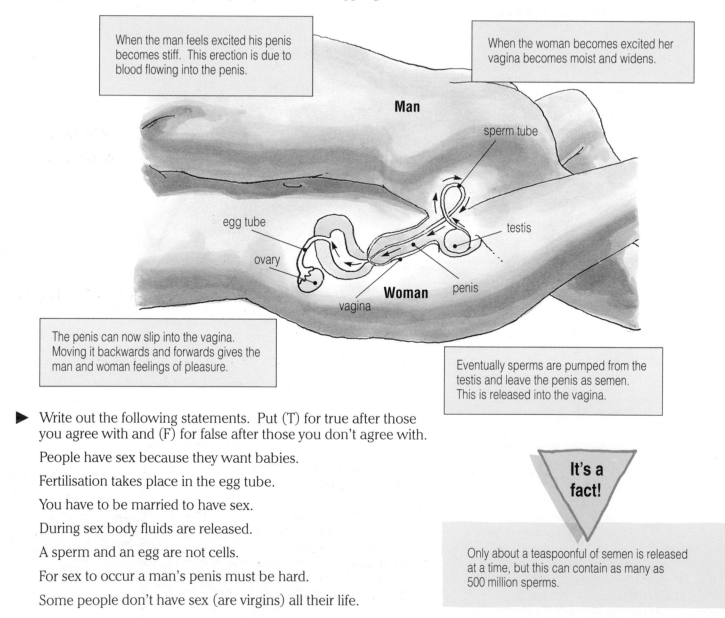

When the man feels excited his penis becomes stiff. This erection is due to blood flowing into the penis.

When the woman becomes excited her vagina becomes moist and widens.

Man

sperm tube

egg tube

testis

ovary

penis

Woman

vagina

The penis can now slip into the vagina. Moving it backwards and forwards gives the man and woman feelings of pleasure.

Eventually sperms are pumped from the testis and leave the penis as semen. This is released into the vagina.

▶ Write out the following statements. Put (T) for true after those you agree with and (F) for false after those you don't agree with.

People have sex because they want babies.

Fertilisation takes place in the egg tube.

You have to be married to have sex.

During sex body fluids are released.

A sperm and an egg are not cells.

For sex to occur a man's penis must be hard.

Some people don't have sex (are virgins) all their life.

It's a fact!

Only about a teaspoonful of semen is released at a time, but this can contain as many as 500 million sperms.

After making love ...

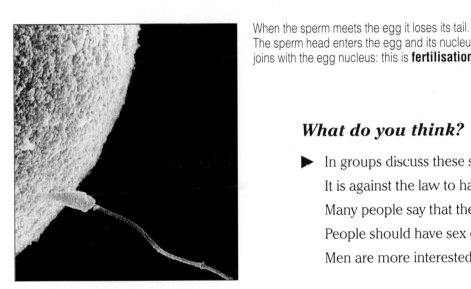

if sperm meets egg in egg tube, fertilisation occurs

one egg released from an ovary every month

sperms swim from vagina up uterus

many sperms die before they reach egg tube

fertilised egg passes down egg tube and settles into uterus. Here it grows into a baby

When the sperm meets the egg it loses its tail. The sperm head enters the egg and its nucleus joins with the egg nucleus: this is **fertilisation**.

What do you think?

▶ In groups discuss these statements:

It is against the law to have sex under the age of 16.

Many people say that they have had sex when they haven't.

People should have sex only if they are in love with each other.

Men are more interested in sex than women.

Not too many

▶ Many societies have their own rules and traditions which help to stop too many children being born. Write about:

• what these rules and traditions are in *your* society

• how they help to control the growth of the population

• rules and traditions used in other countries.

---

1 Copy out and complete the following sentences:
a) Fertilisation is the joining together of ...
b) The sperms are released into ...
c) To get to the egg tube, the sperms swim ...
d) An egg is released from an ovary every ...
e) The fertilised egg passes down the egg tube ...

2 What do you think might happen if the fertilised egg splits into two?

3 Try to explain each of these statements:
a) Fish and frogs produce thousands of eggs into the water.
b) Humans usually produce one egg at a time inside the body of the woman.
c) Men produce millions of sperms.

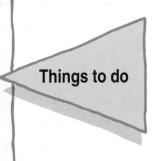

Things to do

Ruth and Jim

Ruth and Jim had wanted a baby for a long time. When Ruth missed her period, they hoped she might be **pregnant**. Ruth went to see her doctor and took along a sample of her urine for a test. After a short time she was told that the test was positive – she was pregnant! She told Jim straight away. They were both so happy and excited at the thought of a baby after waiting for so long.

In the weeks that followed they started to make plans for the new baby. Ruth went to the **ante-natal clinic** regularly. The nurse asked her questions like:
Was it her first pregnancy?
Had she ever had any serious illnesses?
Had there been serious illnesses in her family or in Jim's?
Were there any twins in her family or in Jim's?

Whenever Ruth went to the clinic the nurse weighed her and measured her blood pressure. The midwife or doctor examined her on each visit and she was given lots of advice about how to prepare for the birth of her baby.

▶ Think about Ruth's visits to the ante-natal clinic and answer the following questions.

a Why do you think Ruth was asked about serious illnesses in the family?

b Why was she asked if there were twins in the family?

c Why do you think she was weighed?

d Why do you think her blood pressure was taken?

e Ruth doesn't smoke. Why might the nurse have been worried if she did?

4 weeks

A new life begins

When the fertilised egg passed down Ruth's egg tube, it settled in the thick wall of her uterus. As it grew it eventually formed a **fetus** ('feet-us').

▶ Look at these photographs of the developing fetus inside the uterus:

f What changes can you see? Write them down.

Early in pregnancy, a plate-shaped organ called a **placenta** forms in the uterus. This acts as a barrier stopping infections and harmful substances from reaching the fetus. Inside the placenta the blood of the fetus and the mother come close together. The fetus is attached to the placenta by the **cord**.

▶ Write down your answers to these questions.

g How do you think food and oxygen get to the fetus?

h How do you think the fetus gets rid of waste?

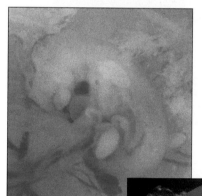

7 weeks

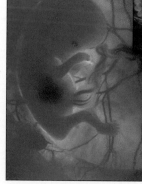

14 weeks

► Look at this diagram of the fetus inside the mother:

i How do you think it is protected during its development?

j Can you see that it is surrounded by a fluid? How do you think this helps the fetus?

Immature thoughts

► Imagine that you are inside the uterus before birth. What is it like?
How do you feed?
How do you breathe?
How are you protected from bumps?
What do you hear?

Write a short story about your experiences.

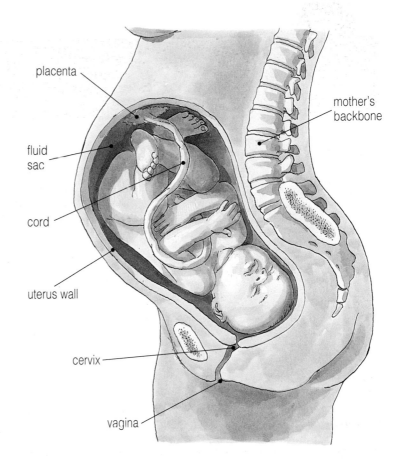

placenta

fluid sac

cord

uterus wall

cervix

vagina

mother's backbone

It's a fact!

The placenta can't act as a barrier to all harmful substances. In the 1960s the drug thalidomide was given to some pregnant women to help them sleep. Some of them gave birth to babies with no arms or legs.

Eating for two

The pregnant mother must eat sensibly. She may be 'eating for two' but that doesn't mean she has to eat twice as much! **Protein** is needed for the baby to grow. It will also need **calcium** for healthy bones and teeth, and **iron** to build up blood cells.

► In your groups, design a poster to show pregnant women that their habits, good and bad, will affect their babies.

It's a fact!

Some germs can get across the placenta to the fetus. If the mother has German measles it can affect the baby's eyes and heart and cause deafness. Twelve-year-old girls are given a rubella injection to stop them catching German measles.

1 What important jobs do each of these do:
a) the placenta?
b) the cord?
c) the fluid sac?

2 What advice would you give to Ruth about keeping healthy during pregnancy?

3 Collect some leaflets or articles giving advice on pregnancy.
Make your own leaflets for an ante-natal clinic.

4 How do you think Jim could have helped Ruth during her pregnancy?
Find out by looking at leaflets and by asking some fathers.

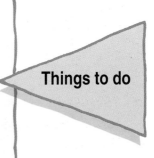

Things to do

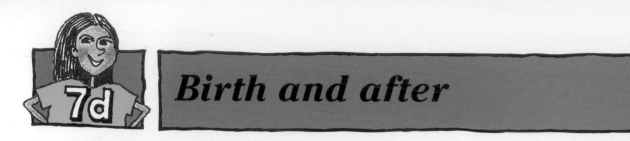

Birth and after

Think about what it is like to be a new-born baby.
How is life outside different from life inside the mother?

▶ Copy and complete this table:

	Inside the uterus	After the birth
How does the baby get food?		
How does the baby get oxygen?		
What sort of things does the baby react to?		
How is the baby protected?		

Ruth's baby

Ruth had been pregnant for 36 weeks.

One day she felt the muscles in her uterus squeezing (**contracting**).
This was the start of **labour**.

Jim took her to the hospital straight away.
He and the **midwife** helped her to get ready for the birth.
Her contractions were getting stronger and coming more often.
Soon the sac of liquid around the baby broke.

After several hours of gradual pushing by Ruth, the baby was born.
It came out head first through her vagina. It was a girl!

She was still joined to Ruth by the cord. The doctor cut this.
Later the rest of the cord and the placenta came out.
This is called the **afterbirth**.

Ruth rested and the baby slept. Soon the baby was hungry.
She had milk from her mother's breasts.
Ruth and Jim decided to call her Laura.

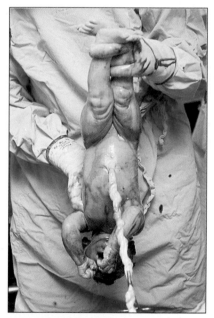

This baby has just been born. The cord is about to be tied and cut.

▶ Write down your answers to the following questions.

a How did the baby come out of Ruth's body?

b What was the cord for?

c Where was your cord joined to your body at birth?

d What is the afterbirth?

Looking after baby

Humans take care of their babies.

▶ When you were a baby you needed things to make you feel happy and safe. You also needed things in order to grow and keep healthy.

Make a list of the things you needed.

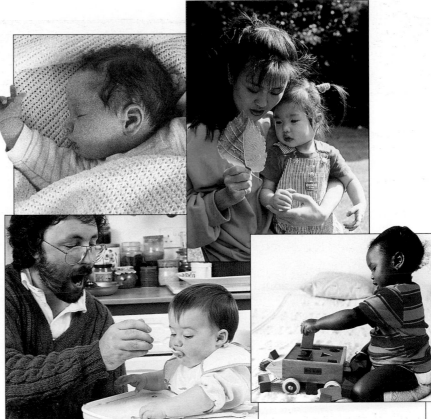

Babies have:
- **physical** needs, like warmth, and
- **emotional** needs, like being loved.

▶ Look at the pictures and see if you can find some of these needs.
Copy and complete this table:

Physical needs	Emotional needs
warmth	being loved

▶ Discuss in groups what you think the following need from their parents:
- a baby
- a 6-year-old
- you.

Left holding the baby

▶ You have been asked to baby sit. Some friends want you to look after Ben, their 18-month-old baby boy for an afternoon.

Write down what you think his physical and emotional needs are.

How can you meet these needs?

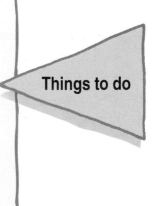

1 Copy and complete:
The baby is ready to be born after . . . . weeks. Normally it is lying . . . . downwards inside the . . . . of the mother. It . . . . out through the mother's . . . . It moves because of . . . . of the wall of the uterus.

2 How do you think Jim could have helped Ruth during the birth of their baby?

3 Mothers take their babies to the clinic for check-ups (post-natal care). What sort of things do you think the nurse would check?

4 Look at the table below.
a) Draw a bar-chart to show the time between fertilisation and birth in the animals listed.
b) Can you see any pattern?

Animal	Time between fertilisation and birth (months)
hamster	0.5
rabbit	1
cat	2
sheep	5
chimpanzee	7
human	9
horse	11
elephant	20

Things to do

Adolescence

Adolescence is a time of change in our lives. During this time each of us changes from a child into a young adult. Our bodies change and so do our emotions.

▶ Have you found a photograph of you when you were 8 or 9 years old? Swap your photograph with that of your friend.

How do you think your friend has changed?

How do you think you've changed?

Puberty is the first stage of adolescence. Most changes in our bodies occur at this time. Not everybody starts puberty at the same time. Girls usually start before boys.

▶ Look at some of the pupils in Years 8 and 9 of your school. Can you see that many of the girls are taller than many of the boys?

If you look at those in Year 11 what do you see? Many of the boys will have caught up with and overtaken the girls.

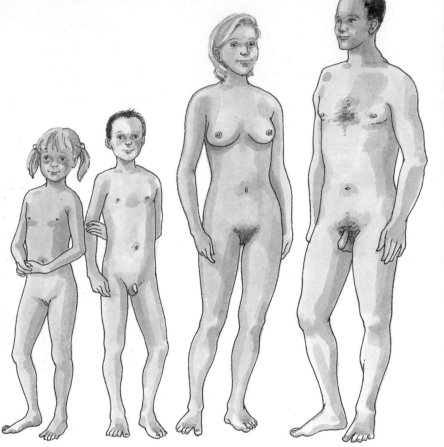

▶ Look at this picture of 9-year-old children and their parents.

a Write down the changes that have taken place between the boy and the man.

b Write down the changes that have taken place between the girl and the woman.

There are some other changes that occur that you can't see in the picture. The table opposite lists some of these changes:

What do you think causes all of these changes?

In a word the answer is '**hormones**'. Hormones are chemicals made in our bodies. Female sex hormones are made by the ovaries. Male sex hormones are made by the testes.

Girls	Boys
ovaries start to release eggs	testes start to make sperms
monthly periods begin	voice becomes deeper ('breaks')

It's a fact!

Many teenagers get spots or acne. This is not due to dirtiness. It's caused by sex hormones and disappears once adolescence is over.

Periods

One change that happens to girls during puberty is they start having periods. So what do we mean by a period?

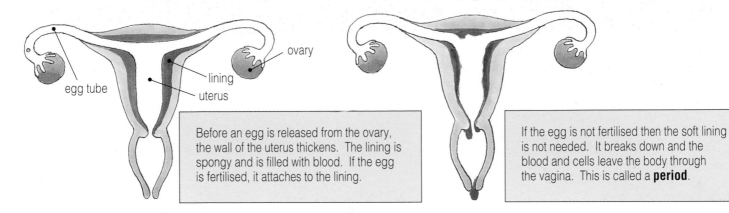

egg tube

ovary

lining

uterus

Before an egg is released from the ovary, the wall of the uterus thickens. The lining is spongy and is filled with blood. If the egg is fertilised, it attaches to the lining.

If the egg is not fertilised then the soft lining is not needed. It breaks down and the blood and cells leave the body through the vagina. This is called a **period**.

A girl's period lasts about 3 to 7 days. Periods usually occur once every 28–31 days, but this can vary. At first periods may be irregular, but as a girl gets older her periods become more regular. Girls can choose sanitary towels or tampons to absorb the flow of blood.

c   What do you think would happen to the lining of the uterus if the egg was fertilised?

Emotions

During adolescence our feelings also start to change.
Suddenly we find the opposite sex more interesting and attractive.
Girls and boys start to look at themselves and ask questions such as:
Am I normal?
Am I too tall or too fat?
Am I attractive to the opposite sex?

▶   In groups, discuss some 'problem letters' written by teenagers.

Do you think the writers are right to be worried?

Write a reply to one of them.

---

1 Copy this diagram and use it to answer the following questions.

Period	Egg released from ovary													Period	

Day 2 4 6 8 10 12 14 16 18 20 22 24 26 28 2 4

a) How often does a period occur?
b) How long does a period last?
c) On which day is an egg released?
d) Mark on your diagram the time when fertilisation is most likely to occur.

2 Why do you think the thick lining of the uterus is needed?

3 An egg is released from a girl's ovary on April 2nd. When will the next egg probably be released:
• April 30th
• May 8th or
• April 14th?

4 Why won't a woman have a period when she is pregnant?

Things to do

Questions

1 a) What happens to human sperms after they are released into the woman's body?

b) What happens to a human egg after it has been fertilised?

2 Do you think that there is any truth in these statements? Write down your reasons in each case.

a) "I've heard that the first time you have sex you can't get pregnant."

b) "If I work out when my egg is released, it is perfectly safe to have sex at other times."

3 Look at this diagram of twin babies inside the uterus:

a) Write down the letters A to D and give the name of each part.

b) What do you think happens to each of these parts during birth?

c) The twin on the right side of the diagram is better placed for birth than the twin on the left. In what way?

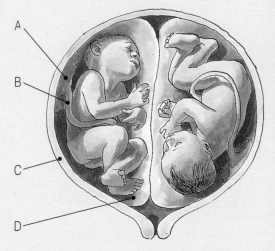

4 How do you think a father can be helpful:

a) during the mother's pregnancy?

b) during the birth?

5 a) Make a list of 4 ways in which a girl's body changes during puberty.

b) Make a list of 4 ways in which a boy's body changes during puberty.

6 Karen is 14. She says:

"I seem to fall out with my parents all the time these days. We argue about where I go, the friends I'm with, even the clothes I wear! We used to get on so well together. Is it my fault? What's happening to me?"

What advice can you give Karen?

7 Mark and Sharon are both 16. They have been going steady for two years. It's Friday night and Sharon has had to go away for the weekend with her parents to a wedding. Mark has nothing to do. His mates call round for him and persuade him to go to the local club disco.

At the disco, Mark notices Joanne. His mates say Joanne has always fancied him …

Write 2 different endings to the story. In one, show that Mark has a caring, responsible attitude towards Sharon. In the other, show that he hasn't.

Magnetism and Electricity

8

Electricity is important to all of us.
Our lives would be very different without it.

We use it for lighting and for heating.

And we can use electricity to make magnets – which we use every day in radios, TVs, cassette players and many other things.

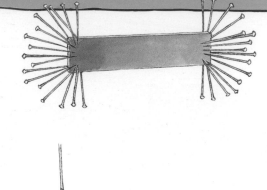

a If you spill some pins on the floor, what is the best way to pick them up?

If you use a magnet, the pins stick to the ends or **poles** of the magnet.

b Can you use a magnet to pick up paper off the floor? Why not?

Sailors used to hang a magnet from a piece of string, so that it could swing freely:

c Why did the sailors do this?

d What is the name of this instrument?

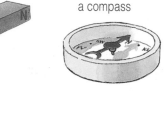

a compass

The end of the magnet that points to the North is called the North-pole (N-pole) of the magnet.

e What is the name given to the other end of the magnet?

Some things are magnetic, and some are not.

f Which of these are magnetic: wood, iron, plastic, paper, steel, rubber, copper, brass?

Making a magnet

A piece of iron or steel can be magnetised by stroking it several times with a magnet:

g Why is it sometimes useful to have a screwdriver which is magnetic?

If a magnet is heated until it is red-hot, it becomes **demagnetised**.

Magnetic fields

Magnets can **attract** (pull) or **repel** (push) other magnets.
A **N**-pole repels another **N**-pole.
A **S**-pole attracts a **N**-pole.

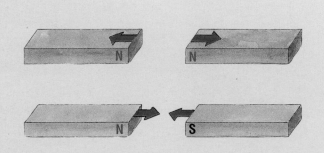

They can do this without touching. This is because a magnet has a **magnetic field** round it. Iron and steel are affected by a magnetic field.

The Earth has a magnetic field round it. This field makes a compass point to the North.

h What happens if a **S**-pole is brought near to a **S**-pole?

Investigating magnetic games

Here are 4 magnetic games. Plan your time carefully to do as many as possible.
For each one, draw a sketch and write down a **scientific** description of what happens.

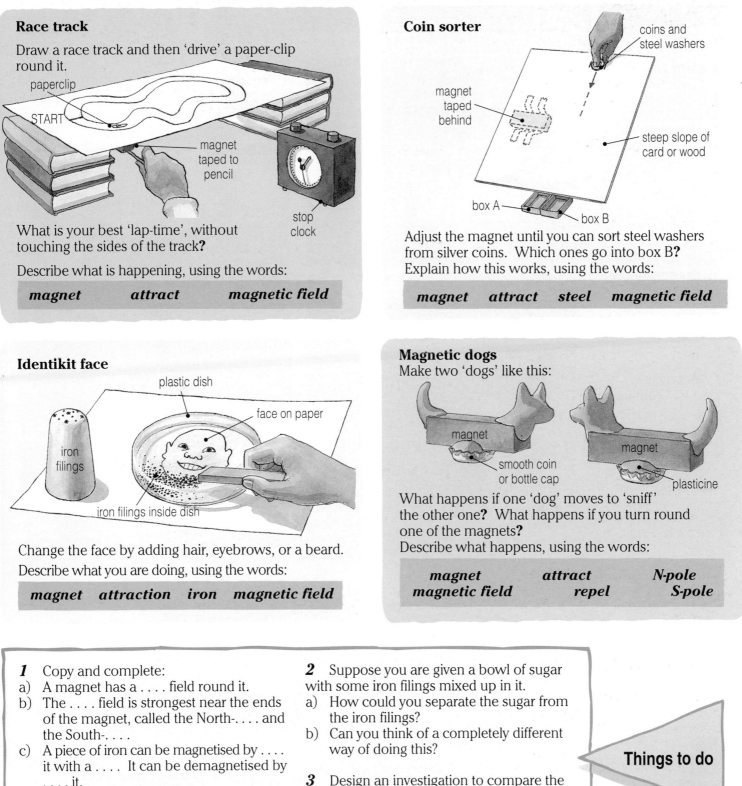

Race track

Draw a race track and then 'drive' a paper-clip round it.

What is your best 'lap-time', without touching the sides of the track?

Describe what is happening, using the words:

magnet	**attract**	**magnetic field**

Coin sorter

Adjust the magnet until you can sort steel washers from silver coins. Which ones go into box B?
Explain how this works, using the words:

magnet	**attract**	**steel**	**magnetic field**

Identikit face

Change the face by adding hair, eyebrows, or a beard.
Describe what you are doing, using the words:

magnet	**attraction**	**iron**	**magnetic field**

Magnetic dogs

Make two 'dogs' like this:

What happens if one 'dog' moves to 'sniff' the other one? What happens if you turn round one of the magnets?
Describe what happens, using the words:

magnet	**attract**	**N-pole**
magnetic field	**repel**	**S-pole**

---

1 Copy and complete:
a) A magnet has a . . . . field round it.
b) The . . . . field is strongest near the ends of the magnet, called the North-. . . . and the South-. . . .
c) A piece of iron can be magnetised by . . . . it with a . . . . It can be demagnetised by . . . . it.
d) The Earth has a magnetic . . . . round it.
e) A N-pole . . . . another N-pole.
A S-pole . . . . a N-pole.

2 Suppose you are given a bowl of sugar with some iron filings mixed up in it.
a) How could you separate the sugar from the iron filings?
b) Can you think of a completely different way of doing this?

3 Design an investigation to compare the strengths of two bar-magnets.
What equipment would you need? Draw a diagram.
How would you make it a fair test?

Things to do

Using magnetic fields

Using magnets

Here are some uses of magnets:

▶ For each one, write down a sentence to describe it. Use these words if you can:

magnet   pole
attract   repel
magnetic field

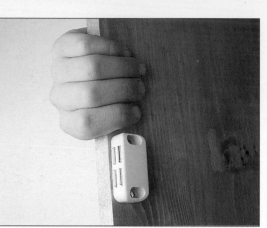

a Cupboard door catch

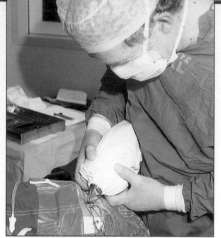

c In an eye hospital

b A compass

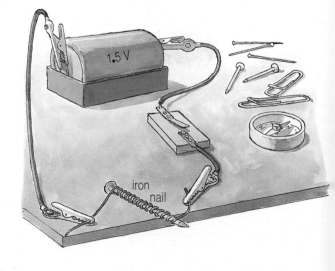

d Magnetic crane in a scrap-yard

Making an electro-magnet

The door-catch and the compass use permanent magnets.
But the crane uses an **electro-magnet**.
An electromagnet can be switched on and off.

1.5 V

iron nail

▶ Use the diagram to make your own electromagnet:

Warning: only connect the battery for a few seconds or it will soon go flat!

● How can you test the strength of your electromagnet? Try it.

● What happens when you switch off the current?

● Can you think how you could make it a stronger magnet? If you have time, try it.

Electromagnets are used in all electric motors, door-bells, loudspeakers and TV sets.

Magnetic fields

We cannot see the magnetic field round a magnet, but we can find out the shape of it.

Put a magnet under a sheet of paper as shown:

Sprinkle some iron filings over the paper and then tap the paper.

Look carefully at the pattern that appears. Can you see that it is the same shape as in the diagram?

Make a sketch of the shape you get.

The iron filings act as tiny compasses, and point along the magnetic field.
The curved lines are called **field lines** or **lines of flux**.

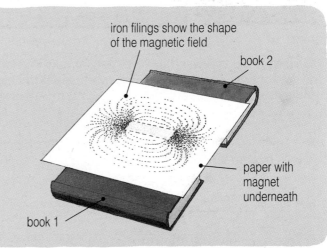

iron filings show the shape of the magnetic field

book 2

paper with magnet underneath

book 1

Here is a better way. Use a *plotting compass* to make a map of the magnetic field.

Follow these instructions carefully.

1   Place your magnet on a large sheet of paper and draw round it to mark its position.

2   Choose a starting point near the N-pole of the magnet and mark it with a pencil dot.

3   Put the 'tail' of the compass pointer over your dot, and then draw a second dot at the 'head' of the compass pointer.

4   Move the compass along until its tail is over this dot, and continue in the same way.

5   Dot the path of the compass as it leads you through the magnetic field. Join up the dots to make a smooth line.

6   Choose another starting point, to get different field lines, as in the diagram.

- Is it the same shape as before?

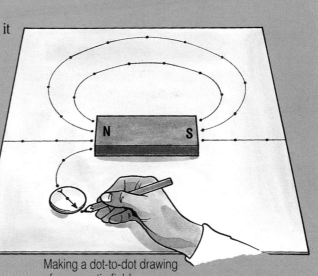

Making a dot-to-dot drawing of a magnetic field

---

1   Make a survey of all the things in your house that use electromagnets.
(Hint: see the bottom of page 98.)

2   Imagine you are a vet, and a dog is brought to you with a steel splinter in its eye. Describe how you might help it.

3   Design a game which uses an electro-magnet.

4   Suppose you wake up tomorrow morning and find that no electro-magnets work any more. Write about how your life would be changed.
(Hint: see the bottom of page 98.)

5   Plan an investigation to see if iron can be made into a magnet more easily than steel. How would you make it a fair test?

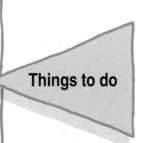

Things to do

Electricity is a very useful way of getting energy. Sometimes we use a **battery** and sometimes we use **mains** electricity. Mains electricity can be dangerous – you must not use it in these experiments.

▶ Make a list of things in your home that use electricity from a battery or from the mains.

▶ Look at the **circuit** shown here.

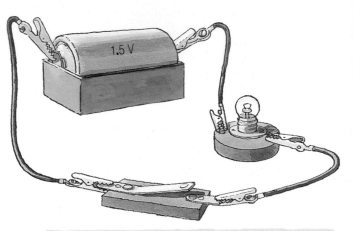

Below it is a **circuit diagram**, which shows the same circuit, in symbols.

Find the symbol for: a) the **battery** (or '**cell**')
                           b) the **lamp bulb**
                           c) the **switch**.

▶ Copy this circuit diagram and label the symbols.

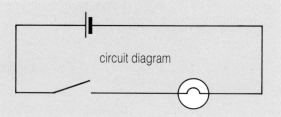

circuit diagram

▶ Now use the equipment to make the circuit.

What do you have to do to make the bulb light up**?**

We say there is an electric **current** flowing in the circuit. A current can flow *only if there is a complete circuit* with no gaps in it.

▶ Look carefully at a switch. What happens when you press it?   How does it work**?**

Conductors and insulators

A material that will let an electric current flow through it is called a **conductor**.
An **insulator** will not let electricity go through it.

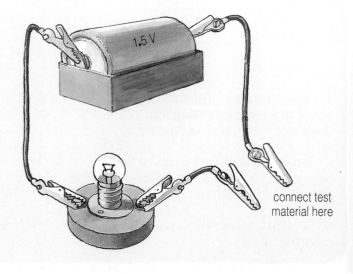

You can use the circuit shown in the diagram to test some materials, to see if they are conductors or insulators.

• Draw a circuit diagram of this circuit.

• Say what would happen when these materials are tested:
   a an iron nail   **b** copper wire   **c** a wooden match
   d a brass key   **e** a 10p coin   **f** a plastic spoon
   g rubber band   **h** paper-clip   **i** pencil   **j** paper.

connect test material here

• Is air a conductor or an insulator? How do you know**?**

Electric games

Choose **one** of these games and draw a detailed diagram of how you would make it.
Show your plan to your teacher, and then make your game.

Steady hand game

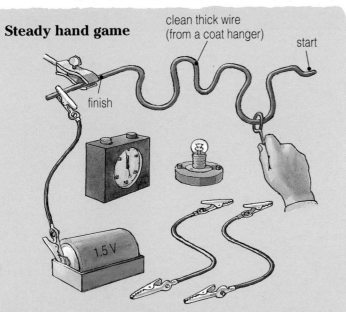

Is your head steady enough for you to be a surgeon or a vet?

- How many seconds does it take you?
- Can you do it with your other hand?
- Can you count backwards from 99 at the same time?

Quiz game

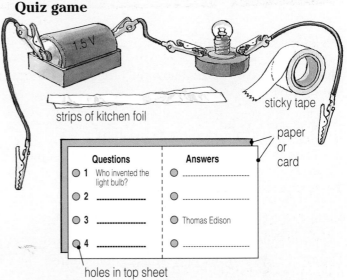

- How can you use the kitchen foil to connect a 'Question' hole to the correct 'Answer' hole (but so it can't be seen)?
- What can you use to insulate the strips of foil from each other?
- Make up your own science questions (and answers) to test your friends.

▶ Write down how your game works, using the words:

battery   connecting wire   complete circuit   electric current   conductor   insulator

---

1 Copy and complete:
a) Mains electricity can be very . . . .
b) When a bulb lights up it shows that an electric . . . . is flowing.
c) For an electric current to flow, there must be a . . . . circuit, with no gaps in it.

2 Answering carefully,
a) Explain what you mean by:
i) a conductor   ii) an insulator.
b) Draw and label the circuit symbols for
i) a battery   ii) a bulb   iii) a switch.
c) Explain what happens when you operate a switch.

3 Suppose you wake up tomorrow morning and find there is no electricity at all in the world. How would your life be different?

4 Mr. Smith is deaf and can't hear his door-bell.
a) Draw a circuit diagram to show how you would connect a bulb to light up when a visitor presses the switch.
b) How would you change it to light another bulb in his kitchen as well as one in his living-room? Draw a circuit diagram.

5 Design a poster to warn young children not to poke at mains sockets or electric fires.

6 Design an investigation to find out if salty water (brine) is a conductor or an insulator.

7 Find out what you can about the life of Michael Faraday.

Things to do

Series and parallel circuits

8d

▶ Look at this diagram:

There is an electric current flowing through the battery and through the wires in the bulb.

a Draw the symbol for a battery, and label it.

b Draw the symbol for a bulb (a lamp).

c Draw this circuit diagram, and mark arrows on it everywhere you think there is a current.

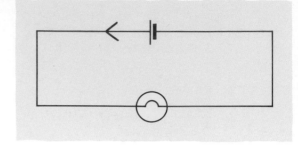

Scientists have discovered that electricity is made up of **electrons**. These are tiny particles, even smaller than atoms. The electrons travel through the wires.

An electric current is rather like water flowing through a pipe. Look at this diagram of the central-heating pipes in a house:

d Which part of the diagram do you think is like a **battery**? (Hint: a battery pushes electrons round a circuit.)

e Which part of the diagram do you think is most like a **bulb**? (Hint: a bulb is heated up by the electrons going through it.)

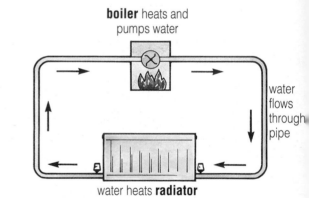

boiler heats and pumps water

water flows through pipe

water heats **radiator**

Series circuit

The water goes through the boiler, and then the same water goes through the radiator.
We say they are **in series**.

In the same way, the electrons go through the battery and then they go through the bulb, and then back to the battery.
It is a **series circuit**.

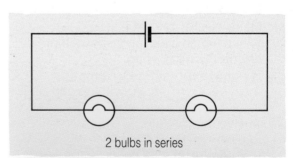

2 bulbs in series

▶ Connect up this series circuit:

f Do both bulbs light up? Is a current going through both bulbs?

g Now unscrew **one** of the bulbs. What happens? Why does this happen?

h Christmas tree lights are often connected in series. What happens then if **one** of the bulbs breaks?

i How do you know that the lights in your house are not wired in series?

Parallel circuits

Look at this circuit, and its circuit diagram below:

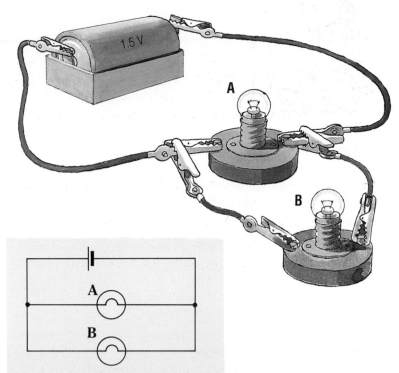

This is a **parallel circuit**.
There are two paths for the current to flow along, with a bulb in each path.
We say the two paths are **in parallel**.

When the electrons travel from the battery, **some** of them go through bulb **A** and **the rest** of them go through bulb **B**.

▶ Connect up this parallel circuit:

j Do both bulbs light up? Is a current going round both paths?

k Now unscrew **one** of the bulbs. Why does the other bulb stay on?

l Are the lights in your house connected in series or in parallel? How do you know?

2 bulbs in parallel

Analysing circuits

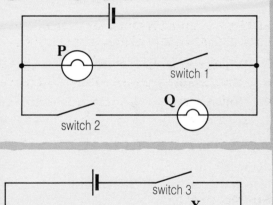

Here is a circuit diagram for 2 lights in a doll's house:

Use your finger to follow the path of the electrons from the battery through the bulb **P** and back to the battery. **If your finger has to go through a switch, then this switch is needed to put on the light.**

m Which switch is needed to switch on bulb **P**?

n Which switch is needed for bulb **Q**?

Use the same method to find out the answers to these questions:

o How would you switch on bulb **X**?

p How would you switch on bulb **Y**?

q Are the bulbs **X** and **Y** connected in series or in parallel?

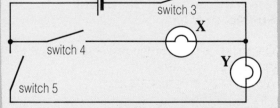

---

1 Copy and complete:
a) In an electric circuit, tiny . . . . move through the wires.
b) If the same current goes through two bulbs, then the bulbs are in . . . .
c) If the current splits up to go through two different paths, we say the paths are in . . . .

2 Design a burglar alarm so that if a burglar steps on your door-mat, an electric bell rings.

3 A torch contains a battery, a switch and a bulb in series.
a) Draw a circuit diagram of this.
Suppose your torch is broken.
b) Describe, with a diagram, how you could test the bulb.
c) How could you test the battery?

4 Jim needs a circuit for his caravan, so that 3 bulbs, each with its own switch, can work from a car battery. Draw a circuit diagram for Jim.

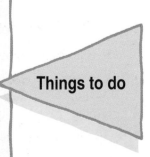

Things to do

We often use electricity to heat things.

▶ Make a list of all the things in your house that use electricity to get hot.

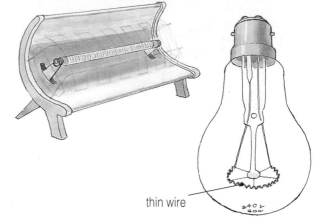

The thin wire inside a light bulb glows white-hot.
This is because the thin wire has a **resistance** to the current.
As the electrons are forced through this thin wire, they heat it up.

An insulator has a very high resistance, and so the current cannot flow. The electrons cannot get through.

A copper wire has a very low resistance. It is a good conductor. The electrons can get through easily.

thin wire

Investigating resistance

Connect up this circuit:

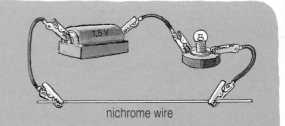

nichrome wire

• What happens when the crocodile clips are close together?
  What happens if you move them apart?

• Write a short report saying what you did and what you found.

Your circuit has a *variable resistance*.
You can vary the amount of resistance it has.

Now look carefully at a **variable resistor**:
How does it work?

Connect the variable resistor to your battery and bulb.

What happens when you move the slider? Why?

Draw a circuit diagram of this circuit.

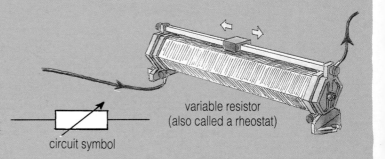

variable resistor
(also called a rheostat)

circuit symbol

Now look at an **ammeter**.
An ammeter measures the size of a current. It measures it in **amperes** (also called **amps** or **A**).

Connect your battery, bulb, variable resistor and an ammeter in series. *Take care* to connect the red (+) terminal on the ammeter to the + (the button) on the battery.

What happens as you vary the resistance?

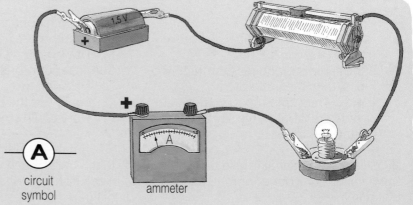

circuit
symbol

ammeter

Fuses for safety

▶ Connect up this circuit:

Put on safety spectacles. Then look carefully at the thin wire while you press the switch. What happens?

▶ Write down what you think is happening, using the words:

> **battery   complete circuit**
> **current   amperes   heating**

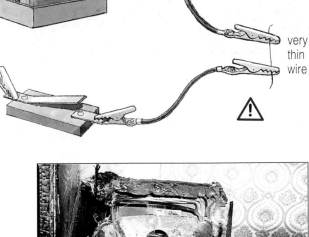

The thin wire has melted or **fused**.
When it fuses, it stops the current flowing.
It is a safety device. We call it a **fuse**.

A fuse is a weak part of the circuit. It breaks if there is a fault which lets too much current flow.

Every mains plug has a fuse inside it.
You can buy fuses with different ratings, such as 3 amp or 13 amp.
A table lamp or TV needs a 3 A fuse.
An electric fire needs a 13 A fuse.

thin wire

3A

13A

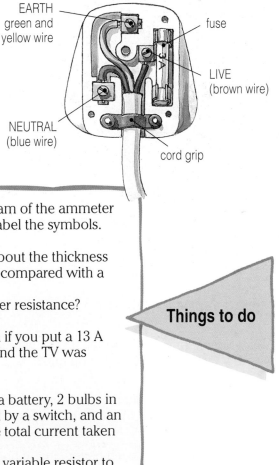

Using the wrong fuse in a TV?

Mains plug

▶ Look carefully at the diagram of a mains plug:
It is very **very** important that the coloured wires are connected to the correct places.

Why is the cord grip important?

▶ Draw a safety poster to help you remember the correct way to wire a plug.

EARTH green and yellow wire

fuse

LIVE (brown wire)

NEUTRAL (blue wire)

cord grip

---

1 Copy and complete:
a) A good conductor has a . . . . resistance. An insulator has a . . . . resistance.
b) The current in a circuit can be varied using a . . . . resistor (also called a . . . .).
c) An ammeter measures the . . . . in a circuit, in . . . . or A.
d) A fuse . . . . if the current is too big.
e) In a mains plug the brown wire is called the . . . . wire and must go to the fuse. The green/yellow wire is the . . . . wire and must go the . . . . pin. The blue wire is the . . . . wire.

2 Where might you use a variable resistor (rheostat) in a theatre? Draw a circuit diagram suitable for a toy theatre.

3 Draw a circuit diagram of the ammeter circuit that you used. Label the symbols.

4 What can you say about the thickness of the wire in a 3 A fuse compared with a 13 A fuse?
Which one has the bigger resistance?

5 What might happen if you put a 13 A fuse in a plug for a TV, and the TV was faulty?

6 Draw a circuit with a battery, 2 bulbs in parallel, each controlled by a switch, and an ammeter measuring the total current taken by the bulbs.
Where would you put a variable resistor to dim one of the bulbs?

Things to do

Batteries are a useful way to make electricity. But expensive!

They have chemicals inside, to store energy.
When you use them in a circuit, the chemical energy is transferred to electrical energy.

▶ Make a list of all the things you can think of that use batteries.

▶ Draw a circuit diagram for a torch.

▶ Draw an Energy Transfer Diagram for a torch.
(Hint: see page 34.)

A battery makes an electric current until the chemicals in it are used up.

Some batteries are **re-chargeable**. They can be re-charged with electricity so that they work again.
A car battery is re-chargeable.

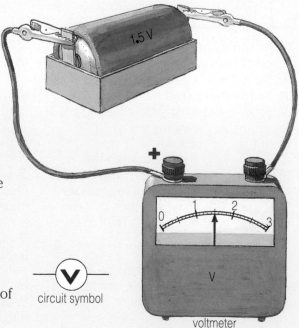

Using a rechargeable battery

A battery pushes electrons round the circuit. The size of the push is measured in **volts**.

Batteries push with just a few volts and are safe.
Mains electricity pushes with 230 volts (230 V) and so it is very dangerous!

Using a voltmeter

Connect a **voltmeter** to a battery. Take care to connect the red (+) terminal of the voltmeter to the + (the button) of the battery. What do you see?

The voltmeter measures how hard the battery pushes the electrons.
What is the voltage of a simple battery (a 'dry cell')?

What do you think will happen if two batteries in series push the **same** way? Try it. What do you find?

What do you think will happen if two batteries in series push in **opposite** directions? Try it. What happens?

What is the voltage of each battery in the photograph at the top of this page?

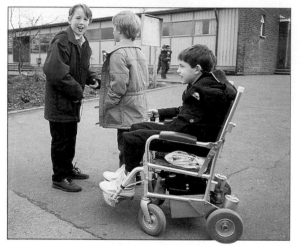

circuit symbol

voltmeter

Fruity batteries

You can make a simple battery by pushing 2 different metals into a fruit:

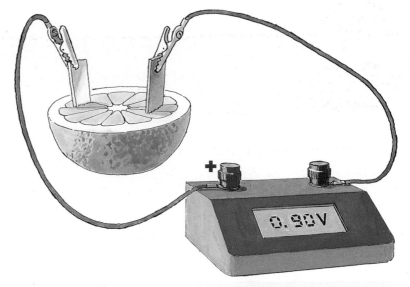

You are going to investigate how to get the highest voltage.

▶ Choose **one** of the investigations.

Then plan it:

- Decide what you are going to change each time.
- Decide what you are going to measure each time.
- Decide what you must keep the same each time, to make it a fair test.
- Decide how to record your results.

Show your plan to your teacher and then do it.

Investigation 1

Which two metals give the highest voltage?

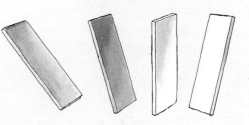

Investigation 2

Which fruit gives the highest voltage?

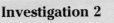

Afterwards:

- Write a report on what you did and what you found out.

- Draw a bar-chart of your results.

- Which gave the highest voltage?

Investigation 3

Which fruit and metals give the highest voltage?

---

1 Copy and complete:
a) A battery pushes . . . . round a circuit. The size of the push is measured in . . . . , by using a . . . .
b) Mains voltage is . . . . volts and so is very . . . .
c) If two 3 volt batteries push together in the same direction, then the total voltage is . . . . volts.

2 Draw a circuit diagram of a battery connected to a voltmeter, with a switch in the circuit.

3 A 9 V battery is made from small 1.5 V batteries. Draw a diagram to explain this.

4 Plan an investigation to find out if it is better value to buy a cheap battery or a 'long-life' battery.

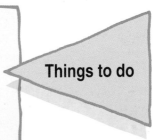

Things to do

Questions

1 Design a 'magnetic fishing game' for young children.
You could use a magnet, paper-clips, card, string and a stick.
Draw a diagram and make a set of rules for the game.

2 Design a poster to warn children against climbing electric pylons or going on to electric railway lines.

3 Draw a labelled diagram of a light bulb.
Which parts are: a) insulators?   b) conductors?

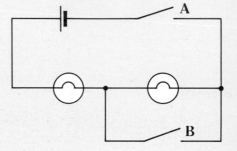

4 In the circuit shown in the diagram, what happens if:
a)   switch **A** only is closed?
b)   switch **B** only is closed?
c)   **A** and **B** are closed?
d)   Are the bulbs in series or in parallel?

5 a)   An electric saw needs 2 switches for safety.
Design a circuit so that both switches must be 'on' to start the saw, but only one switch need be turned 'off' to stop the saw.
b)   A bank needs an alarm system.
Design a circuit that has a battery and an alarm bell that can be switched on by 2 separate push-buttons.
c)   Which of these two circuits (a or b) could you use for door-bell switches at your front door and back door?

6 This diagram shows one kind of ammeter.
What are the readings **a**, **b**, **c**, **d**?

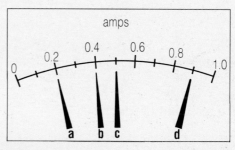

7 Draw a circuit diagram to show how two 6 volt bulbs can be lit brightly from two 3 volt batteries.

8 Each of the pictures below shows an unsafe situation.
For each one:
i)   write a sentence about what is wrong, and
ii)   say what should be done to make it safe.

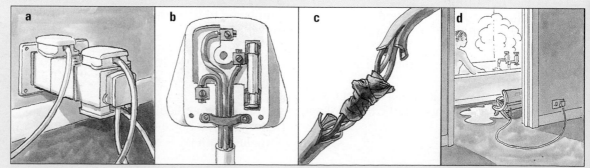

Matter

The Eiffel Tower in Paris is about 300 metres high.
But did you know its height can change?
In summer it is taller than in winter.
The difference can be 10 cm.
Finding out about matter might help to explain why ...

Solids, liquids and gases

▶ Look at these photographs of substances you might find at home.

Which are solids? Which are liquids?
Which are gases?

Make a table to show your answers.

You might be able to tell easily which things are solids, which are liquids and which are gases. It can be hard to explain **how** you can tell!

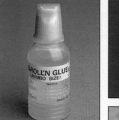

▶ Observe the samples your teacher will give you.
In your group write down some differences between the way solids, liquids and gases behave.

Make a table to show your answers. These are the **properties** of solids, liquids and gases.

Some substances are difficult to classify.

Think about custard!

You can have liquid custard.
It's easy to pour.
It can be stirred.
It takes the shape of its container.

When custard sets it behaves like a solid.
It cannot be poured.
It cannot be stirred.
It has its own shape.

Is custard solid or liquid?

▶ Look at the instructions for making instant custard:

a   How do you think you could make the custard thicker?

b   How could you make the custard more runny?

c   How could you make sure the custard is smooth?

Empty one sachet into a measuring jug.
Add BOILING WATER to $\frac{3}{4}$ pint (425 ml) mark.

Looking at solids, liquids and gases

Squashing

- Put the top tightly on a plastic bottle filled with air.
  Squeeze the bottle with your hands.
  Can you squash the bottle inwards?

- Now fill the plastic bottle with water.
  Put the top on tightly again.
  Try to squeeze the bottle.

- Take a piece of rock. Squeeze it with your hands.

d   What do you notice? Try to explain your results.

e   What do they tell you about solids, liquids and gases?

Watching

- Drop a crystal in a beaker of water.
  Leave it for a while. Watch.

f   What do you notice? Try to explain your results.

g   What do they tell you about solids and liquids?

Smelling

- Take the top off the bottle your teacher will give you.
  Hold it 10 cm away from you.

h   What do you notice? Try to explain your results.

i   What do they tell you about gases?

▶   Look at your table about how solids, liquids and gases behave.
Can you add some more ideas to the table now?

---

1   Fill in the blanks with either 'liquids' or 'solids'.

. . . . are runny.
. . . . are hard.
. . . . can be poured.
. . . . take the shape of the container.
. . . . cannot be stirred.
. . . . have a fixed shape.
. . . . and . . . . cannot be easily squashed.

2   Some substances are difficult to classify as liquids or solids. Custard is one example. Write down 3 other examples.

3   Write a paragraph about liquids. Include the following words:

> wet   pour   thick   thin   drip
> flow   container   freeze

4   Write a paragraph about gases. Include the following words:

> squash   air   smell   light
> fizzy   balloon

Things to do

111

In a state

You can describe substances as **solids**, **liquids** and **gases**.
These are the 3 **states of matter**.

Which is
. . .the solid?
. . .the liquid?
. . .the gas?

Particles

You have already seen that solids, liquids and gases behave in different ways.

We can explain the differences using a theory.
Scientists believe that everything is made of tiny **particles**.

In solids, liquids and gases the particles are arranged in different ways.

The 3 drawings opposite represent the 3 ways:

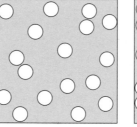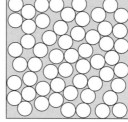

▶ In your group discuss which drawing represents:
  • a solid
  • a liquid
  • a gas.

  Your table of solid, liquid and gas properties should help you to decide.

  Check your ideas with your teacher.

▶ Copy the particle arrangements shown above.
  Label each one as either solid, liquid or gas.

  Do you think particles move   … in solids?
                                 … in liquids?
                                 … in gases?

  Give reasons for your ideas.

Warming a solid

What happens to the length of a wire when it is heated?

Predict what will happen in the experiment shown opposite.

Now try it out.

⚠ Care – hot wires can burn.

Warm the wire with a Bunsen burner.

What happens to the length of the wire?

Use the idea of *particles* to explain what you see.

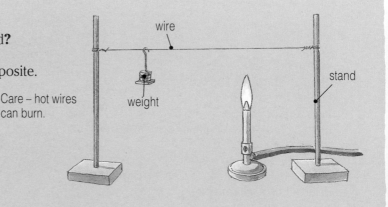

Warming a liquid

Fill a test-tube with water.
Put a rubber stopper and glass tube in it, as shown in the diagram opposite.
Mark the water level above the stopper.

Predict what will happen when the tube is put in a beaker of hot water.

Now try it out.

What happens to the volume of a liquid when it is warmed?

What happens when the liquid is cooled again?

Use the idea of **particles** to explain what you see.

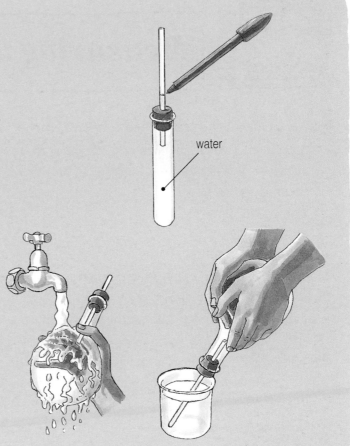

water

Warming a gas

Predict what you think will happen in this experiment.

Take a flask fitted with a stopper and a glass tube.
Run cold water on to the outside for 3 minutes.
Put the glass tube into a beaker of water.
Warm the outside of the flask with your hands.

Now try the experiment.

Use the idea of **particles** to explain what you see.

When things get bigger, we say they **expand**.
When things get smaller, we say they **contract**.

Gases, liquids and solids **expand** when heated.

a Which expands most, a gas, a liquid or a solid?

Things to do

1 Copy and complete using some of the words in the box:

melting	lumps	large	small
solids	gases	liquids	particles
same	contract	hot	expand

a) The three states of matter are . . . . , ... and . . . .
b) . . . . and . . . . are harder to compress (squeeze together) than . . . .
c) Everything is made of . . . .
d) The particles are very . . . .
e) Oven shelves fit more tightly in . . . . ovens.
f) Gases, liquids and solids . . . . when warmed.

2 Which of the following is the best substance to use to fill bicycle tyres? Why?

water	compressed air	wood

3 The label on a lemonade bottle shows the contents:

water, citric acid, flavourings, carbon dioxide, artificial sweetener

a) Name one substance in the list that is:
   i) a liquid   ii) a gas.
b) There is normally a lot of sugar in fizzy drinks. Which substance in the list replaces sugar?
c) Why do you think that sugar is not used here?
d) Is sugar a solid, liquid or gas?

113

Measuring with solids and liquids

▶ Check the following statements.

Say whether you think each one is **true** or **false**.

Explain your answer in each case.

Discuss your answers with the others in your group.
Can you all agree?

- Solids are denser than gases.
- It takes more time to measure the mass of shampoo than the mass of a wooden block.
- It takes more time to measure the volume of a piece of rock than the volume of some water.
- A piece of rock is always heavier than a piece of plastic.
- Water is heavier when it turns to solid ice.

Are solids denser than gases?

Melting

If you heat a solid, you can turn it into a liquid.
We say that the solid **melts**.

▶ Make a list of 6 things you have seen melt, e.g. butter, …

The temperature when a solid melts (turns to liquid) is called the **melting point**.

This is the same temperature as when the liquid freezes (turns to solid).

This temperature is also called the **freezing point**.

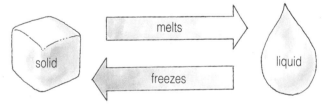

▶ Look at the melting point values in the table.

a Which substance has the lowest melting point?

b Which substance has the highest melting point?

c In cold weather, which freezes first, water or alcohol?

d Room temperature is about 25 °C. Which of these substances may be liquids at this temperature? Why can't you be sure?

e On being heated from room temperature, which melts first, aluminium or copper?

f What happens if you keep heating a liquid?

g What happens to the particles when a solid melts?

Substance	Melting point in °C
aluminium	660
ice	0
alcohol	−117
iron	1535
copper	1083
mercury	−39
polythene	110

Why do we put salt on roads in winter?

To answer this question you could use some temperature sensors.

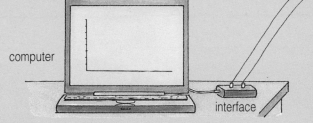

computer

interface

ice   ice and salt

- Place the sensors on the desk carefully.
- Get 2 boiling tubes. Put 10 g of crushed ice into each.
- Add 0.2 g of salt to one tube and stir to mix the ice and salt completely.
- Quickly put one temperature sensor in each tube.
  Make sure it is in the centre of the crushed ice. Wait 1 minute.
- Record the temperature of the ice for 20 minutes.
- Watch the ice carefully.
  Record any changes in its appearance over the 20 minutes.

Draw or print out the graph to show how the temperature changes.
Mark on your graph the point at which the ice melted.

h At the start, what was the **state** of the ice?

i What happened to the solid ice after a while?

j Are the graphs for 'ice on its own' and 'ice and salt' different in any way?

k Describe the shape of the graphs. Which part of the graphs is surprising?

l What effect does salt have on ice?

m Why is salt put on roads in winter?

---

1 Copy and complete each of these statements using one of the words in brackets at the end.
a) Solids are . . . . dense than gases. (less/more)
b) The . . . . when a solid melts is called the melting point. (temperature/time)
c) The . . . . of a liquid is measured in cm³. (mass/volume)
d) When a solid melts it forms . . . . (ice/liquid)
e) When a liquid freezes it turns to . . . . (solid/gas)

2 Cooking oil and alcohol expand when they are heated.
Design an investigation to see which liquid expands more.

3 Explain how you can measure the density of a piece of rock

$$\left(\text{density} = \frac{\text{mass}}{\text{volume}}\right)$$

Use diagrams to help you explain.

4 Explain why **liquids** are used in thermometers.

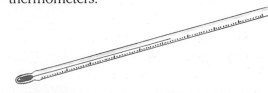

5 Use the information in the melting point table opposite to draw a bar-chart. Organize the substances in melting point order for your bar-chart.

Things to do

What a gas!

Gases are all around you.
The air you are breathing is a gas.
Gases fill any space they are put into.
Gases are made when liquids boil.

LIQUID $\xrightleftharpoons[\text{condenses}]{\text{boils}}$ GAS

The temperature when a liquid boils is called the **boiling point**.

Gases
hydrogen
oxygen
air
nitrogen
carbon dioxide
chlorine
helium
neon
ozone
carbon monoxide

▶ Some gases are listed in the box opposite.
What do you know about them?
Make a patterned note to show your ideas.
You could start like this:

breathe air
oxygen

GASES

Use books and ROMs to find extra information.

Two important gases make up most of the air. About 78% of the air is **nitrogen**. About 21% is **oxygen**. The rest of the air is made up of other gases such as carbon dioxide and helium.

Gases are much lighter than solids and liquids.
Different gases have different masses.
Nitrogen is slightly lighter than oxygen. Helium is a very light gas.
Carbon dioxide is a heavy gas.

Where is the air?

▶ You cannot see the gases in the air.
How do you know the air is all around you?

. Discuss this in your group.

Use these photographs to help you with your ideas.

Where is the air?

Making oxygen

The most important gas in the air is **oxygen**.
We need it to breathe. It keeps us alive.

In this experiment you can make some oxygen gas.
You can also test to prove it is there!

Your teacher will show you how to
'collect a gas over water'.

- Put 2 spatula measures of the black
  powder into a conical flask.

- Fit a stopper, a thistle funnel and a
  delivery tube into the flask, as shown in
  the diagram.

- Fill some test-tubes with water.
  You will use these to collect the oxygen.

- Set up your apparatus to collect the gas.

- Pour hydrogen peroxide down the thistle
  funnel.
  **Do not collect the first few bubbles
  of gas. Why not?**

- Collect 2 or 3 tubes of oxygen gas.
  Put a stopper in each tube.
  Put the tubes in a test-tube rack.

- Light a spill.
  Blow it out so that the tip is glowing.

- Put the glowing spill inside the tube.
  What do you see?

- Draw a picture to show how the particles
  are arranged in the oxygen.

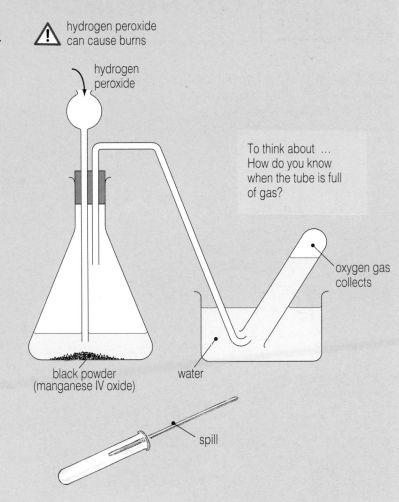

⚠ hydrogen peroxide
can cause burns

hydrogen
peroxide

To think about …
How do you know
when the tube is full
of gas?

oxygen gas
collects

black powder
(manganese IV oxide)

water

spill

1 Copy and complete:
a) The air is made up of 2 main gases
   called . . . . and . . . .
b) . . . . is the gas we use to breathe.
c) We breathe out a gas called . . . . dioxide.
d) Helium is a very . . . . gas.
e) We cannot describe the shape of a gas
   because . . . .

2 Laura has drunk all the lemonade in her
bottle. She says the bottle is empty.
Is she right?

3 Which is heavier?

air   oxygen

Explain your idea.

4 Jill has 3 balloons which are filled with
different gases.
Which balloon holds:
a) air?
b) helium?
c) carbon dioxide?

5 Draw a pie-chart to show the
composition of the air.
Label the sections 'oxygen', 'nitrogen' and
'other gases'.

Things to do

On the move

gas

What did you decide about particles? Can they move?
Scientists think that particles move.

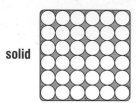

solid

Particles in a solid are close together. They do not move about but they do vibrate.

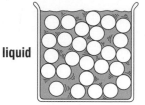

liquid

Particles in a liquid move about. They are still quite close together.

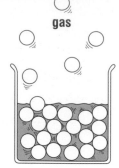

Particles in a gas move about quickly. They move in all directions. They are further away from each other.

▶ Look at these pictures. They all give clues about gas particles moving.

picture 1

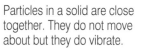

picture 2

PETROLEUM SPIRIT HIGHLY FLAMMABLE

NO SMOKING

picture 3

TANKER CRASH LATEST

The tanker was carrying ammonia. The gas can affect eyes and breathing. People living within a 3 mile radius of the crash were moved from their homes.

picture 4

The pictures tell you that gas particles can move and mix.
They do this without being stirred or shaken.
This is called **diffusion**.
We say that gases **diffuse**. We could also say "The smell of perfume is **diffusing** throughout the room".

a Write about 2 lines to say what is happening to the gas particles in picture 1.

b The roses in picture 2 smell lovely. Draw them and show how their smell spreads in a room. Use dots to represent particles. (Hint: lots of dots together mean a strong smell.)

c Why is 'No smoking' important at the petrol station in picture 3?

d Look at picture 4. Why did people living 3 miles from the crash have to be moved?

e Think of some tests you could carry out to see if liquids or solids diffuse.
Write down:
- what you would do
- how you would know about any diffusion.

No confusion – it's **diffusion**

Where has it gone?

When some solids are put into a liquid like water, they get smaller.
Some solids disappear.
If the solid disappears, we say it has **dissolved**.

The liquid we get when a solid dissolves is a **solution**.

▶ Think about particles on the move.
Discuss these questions in your group.

- Why does sugar dissolve when you put it into a cup of tea?
- Where do the sugar particles go?
- Does sugar dissolve faster in cold tea or hot tea?
- Do sugar particles move faster in cold tea or hot tea?

Investigating solutions

Jawad was investigating solutions.

He filled a beaker to the 200 cm³ mark with water.

He then used a balance to find the mass of beaker + water.

Mass of beaker + water = __ g

He added sugar granules to the water. He stirred the water until he could not see the sugar. It had dissolved.

He used the balance to find the mass of beaker + sugar solution.

Mass of beaker + sugar solution = __ g

f Predict Jawad's results:
do you think the mass will stay the same?
… get smaller?
… get bigger?

g Why did you choose this answer?

Now try Jawad's experiment for yourself.

h What do you find?

---

1 Match each of the following descriptions with the correct word.

	Description	Word
a)	solid disappearing in a liquid	diffusing
b)	particles moving and mixing	predicting
c)	the liquid made when a solid dissolves	mass
d)	saying what you think will happen	solution
e)	a measurement made in grams	dissolving

2 Look at the contents of the cupboards in your kitchen.
Do any of the labels or containers talk about dissolving?
Make a note of what is said.

Product	Notes on dissolving
oven cleaner	dissolves grease and baked on food

3 Think about dissolving a sugar cube in water. What could you do to make it dissolve faster?
List your ideas.

Things to do

Do you have a solution?

Penny, Mike and Chung were talking about **dissolving** things.

Who do you think was right?

▶ Imagine you are the pupils' teacher.

Try to help this group understand melting and dissolving.

Write down what you would say to each person.

Making a solution

In this experiment you can test some solids to see if they dissolve in water.

- Half fill a test-tube with water.

- Add 1 spatula measure of solid to the water.

- Shake the tube gently for 1 minute.

- Look to see if any of the solid has disappeared.
  If so, it must have **dissolved**.

- Do the experiment again with other solids.

Solids which dissolve are said to be **soluble**.

Solids which do not dissolve are said to be **insoluble**.

a   Which solids are soluble in water?

b   Which solids are insoluble in water?

c   Penny says "You can use this experiment to see which substance is the most soluble."
    Is she right?
    Give Penny some advice on how she could improve the experiment.

Sometimes it is hard to tell if a solid has dissolved.

d   How could you test to see if any solid has dissolved?

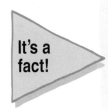
In 1949 a man was charged with murder. He had dissolved his victim's body in concentrated sulphuric acid. He thought he could not be found guilty because there was no body.

... But sulphuric acid does not dissolve everything. The police found the victim's false tooth. The 'acid bath murderer' was found guilty!

Think about dissolving

Do you remember about hypotheses?
(Look back to page 14.)
These are ideas about things which always happen.

You can make a hypothesis.
From this you can make a **prediction**.
Then you can collect evidence
to see if it is true.

Mike had a hypothesis about dissolving.
He said "I think substances always dissolve faster if they are stirred."
Do you think he was right?

Think about *your own* work on dissolving.
Write down your own hypothesis about dissolving.
Use your ideas about particles to predict what will happen.

Plan an investigation to test your prediction.

How can you make your results reliable?

Ask your teacher if you can carry out your investigation.

1 Copy and complete:
a) Solids which dissolve are called . . . . solids.
b) . . . . solids do not dissolve.
c) A solid is said to dissolve if it . . . . when put in water.

2 Plan an investigation to test Mike's idea about dissolving.

3 Draw particle diagrams to show what you think happens when:
a) a solid melts
b) a solid dissolves in water.

4 Look carefully at the wordsquare. Find as many words as you can about this topic. You should be able to find 11.
Do not mark this book.

D	F	D	Y	M	L	S	C
I	H	I	M	E	O	Z	E
F	G	S	O	L	I	D	X
F	A	S	V	T	E	B	P
U	S	O	E	S	V	B	A
S	O	L	U	T	I	O	N
E	P	V	M	I	X	I	D
J	W	E	D	R	O	L	T

Things to do

Questions

1 Imagine you are the teacher of a class of 10-year-olds.
Think about some tests your pupils could do to
classify things as solids or liquids.

Design a worksheet which shows:
- the apparatus pupils need
- clear instructions for each test
- the results expected for solids
- the results expected for liquids.

Make sure your worksheet is interesting!
You could draw diagrams, cartoons or pictures on it.
You could even set some homework!

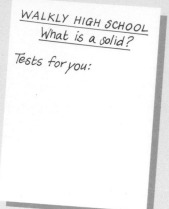

WALKLY HIGH SCHOOL
What is a solid?

Tests for you:

2 Write a paragraph about solids using the following words:

> stir   pour   shape   melt   contract
> freeze   water   ice   expand

3 Choose one of the gases you know about.
Design a poster for 10-year-old children to tell them about
this gas and its uses.

4 Plan an investigation to find out how much gas is given
off by one can of fizzy drink.

5 Explain each of the following statements.
a) Heating a metal top on a glass jar helps
   you to remove the top.
b) The Eiffel Tower is smaller in winter
   than in summer.
c) Icing on a cake can run.

6 A purple crystal is put into a beaker of water.
It starts to dissolve.
Draw pictures to show what you think will be seen:
a) after 10 minutes   b) after 2 hours   c) after 2 weeks.

7 Design an investigation to show how the temperature of the water
affects the speed at which a solid dissolves in it.

8 What makes a good group discussion?
In this topic you have discussed lots of ideas and problems.
Draw up a set of points to look for, which your teacher could use to
judge how well you discuss.

Environment

What is your environment?

It includes your house, your school, your street – in fact, all of your surroundings.

Animals and plants are affected by their environment.

This topic is about how living things depend upon their environment for their survival.

sparrowhawk

caterpillar

butterfly

oak leaves

squirrel

jay

acorn

robin

badger

bee

mushrooms

stoat

grass snake

grass

lichen

primrose

frog

fly   toad

slug

bank vole

blackberries

foxglove

A place to live

The place in which a plant or animal lives is called its **habitat**. The **habitat** must provide everything that the living thing needs to survive.

▶ Your house is part of your habitat. What does it provide for you**?**

▶ Make a list of some things that animals need to survive. Make a list of some things that plants need to survive.

▶ Look at the photographs and write down how each living thing is able to survive in its own habitat.

Cactus plants live in dry habitats. Their leaves are sharp spines. They store water inside their thick stems.

Water boatmen live in ponds. They often swim to the surface of the water.

Many woodland birds build their nests in holes in trees.

Angler fish live in the deep sea. No plants live there as it is always dark.

How do small animals survive?

Small animals live in habitats around your school. Because they live there successfully we say that they are **adapted** to the habitat. They will not be easy to see. Many small creatures hide in long grass, under leaves and in cracks in bark or rocks. Many come out only at night. Here are some ways of finding animals. Choose the one that best suits the habitat.

Pooters

These are small containers with two tubes attached. You suck in through one tube and point the other at the small animal you want to collect. The gauze makes sure you don't get a mouthful of insect. Make sure you suck through the right tube!

My goodness! It's windy today!

Sweep nets

Many insects hide in long grass. A strong net is swept through the grass about 10 times so that the insects drop off into the net bag. You can use a pooter to collect them from the bag.

Uh-uh!

Tree beating

Trees and bushes provide food for many small animals. You can collect them by placing a white sheet under a branch. Shake or bang the branch with a stick so that the animals fall out. Take care not to damage the branch. Collect the animals with a pooter.

Pitfall traps

You can set yoghurt pots into holes in the ground. The rim of the pot must be level with the soil surface.

Look at the picture. How do you think small animals get trapped?

Don't sink the rim below soil level or water may enter. Pitfall traps should be left overnight.

▶ Use a hand lens to study the animals that you have collected.

Be very careful not to damage them.

Your teacher will give you a sheet to help you find out their names.

▶ Where exactly are they found? Do they live on particular food plants? Are they well camouflaged? If so why?

What conditions do they like to live in?

Do they prefer light or dark? Dry or damp?

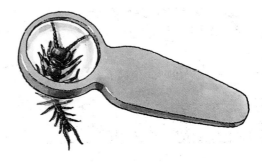

▶ Record your findings in a table like this:

Name of animal	Number in sample	How is it adapted to living in its habitat?
Centipede	2	Moves very fast on many legs. Has large jaws.

Return all animals, unharmed, to where you found them.

Things to do

1 Match up the following living things with their correct habitats:

moss	pond
trout	hedge
squirrel	path
frog	stream
dandelion	wall
hawthorn	wood

2 List some conditions that make life difficult in the following habitats:
a) stream   c) seashore rock-pool
b) hedge   d) mountain.

3 Explorers have been able to survive in very bad conditions. How have they stayed alive:
a) in outer space?
b) at the bottom of the sea?
c) in the frozen Arctic?

4 Write a letter to your pen friend on the planet Zorgan. Explain what conditions are like on Earth. Talk about your own habitat and the animals and plants that share it with you.

Changing seasons

A

B

C

D

We notice the weather getting colder in the winter and we put on warmer clothes. But how do animals and plants survive the changes?

▶ Look at these 4 photographs. Discuss with the others in your group which photograph was taken in which season. Give reasons for your choice.

Plants in winter

A garden in winter looks very bare compared with in summer. Many plants seem to have disappeared. Many of those that you can see have lost all their leaves. Why do you think this is?

Many plants survive the winter as seeds in the ground. What happens to these in the next spring or summer?

▶ Look at this picture of a daffodil. How do you think it is able to stay alive below the ground in winter?

Many trees lose their leaves in order to survive in winter. They grow new leaves in the spring.

▶ List three trees that lose their leaves in winter. List three trees or shrubs that keep their leaves all year round. Look at some of these leaves. Write down your ideas about why they're good leaves for winter.

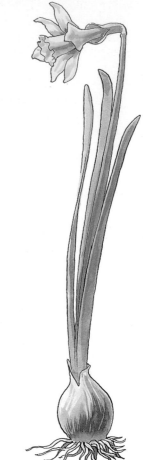

Shivering seeds!

Gardeners usually sow pea seeds at the end of the spring. They do this so that the young pea plants are not killed by frost. The plants grow and the new peas can be picked in the summer.

Some new varieties of pea seeds are able to survive frost. This means that they can be sown earlier in the year. Why would this be useful to the gardener?

Plan an investigation to find out how well seeds survive frost.

Remember that you must make it a fair test.

What other conditions might affect the growth of the seeds?

How long will your investigation take?

Think how you are going to record your results.

Show your plan to your teacher.

Then start your investigation.

126

Hibernation

Do you know where all the greenfly go in winter? They lay eggs with a very tough coat to help them to survive the cold. The old greenfly then die and the new greenfly hatch out in the spring.

Ladybirds feed on greenfly, but in the winter they have no food. So ladybirds **hibernate** in cracks in bark and under dead leaves.

Many small animals like hedgehogs, squirrels, dormice and frogs hibernate. They eat a lot towards the end of the summer and build up a layer of fat under their skin. Then they find a quiet spot and go to sleep for the winter.

▶ Write down your answers to these questions.

a Give some reasons why animals hibernate.

b How are they able to go without food for so long?

c What do you think will happen to the fat layer during the winter?

Migration

Have you seen birds flying off in the autumn? Swallows and martins escape the winter by flying to warmer countries. This is called **migration**.

▶ List some of the problems that birds face in winter.

Some birds visit Britain in the winter. Birds like Bewick's swans and pink-footed geese arrive in this country in the autumn. They come from the colder north and escape even harsher conditions found there.

▶ Look at the map showing the migration routes of 4 birds.

d Which two birds do you think are summer visitors to Britain?

e Which do you think are winter visitors to Britain?

---

1 How do each of the following pass the winter:
a) hedgehog?
b) swallow?
c) greenfly?
d) Bewick's swan?

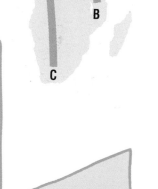

2 Some animals undergo changes in order to survive the winter.
a) Some animals like the stoat and birds like the ptarmigan have white coats in winter. Why do you think this is?
b) Many wild animals grow thick coats in winter. So do cats and dogs. Why do you think this is?

3 Discuss how you could help garden birds to survive the winter. Make a poster to encourage others to care for birds in winter.

4 Different climates have different patterns of rainfall throughout the year.
a) Plot 2 graphs using the following sets of rainfall data.

Month	Rainfall in mm	
Jan	55	60
Feb	50	80
Mar	30	170
Apr	20	250
May	15	23
June	5	120
July	0	80
Aug	0	80
Sept	20	90
Oct	20	90
Nov	50	140
Dec	60	130

b) Study the rainfall patterns shown and label your graphs with either Entebbe (tropical forest) or Alice Springs (hot desert).

Things to do

Who's eating who?

Why do you think cows, horses and sheep spend so much time eating? They eat mainly grass.
Animals that eat plants are called **herbivores**.

▶ Make a list of some other herbivores.

Animals such as lions, owls and foxes feed on meat.
We call animals that eat other animals **carnivores**.

▶ Make a list of some other carnivores.

How do you think plants feed?
Green plants get their energy from the Sun. They are able to change light energy into chemical energy in food. They are the only living things able to do this. Green plants are called **producers**.

Food chains

A **food chain** shows the movement of energy between plants and animals.

GRASS ———— (eaten by) ————▶ RABBIT ———— (eaten by) ————▶ FOX

The arrows show the direction in which the energy flows from one to another.

Here is a food chain with 4 links:

GRASS ————▶ GRASSHOPPER ————▶ FIELDMOUSE ————▶ OWL

Notice that the food chain always begins with a producer (green plant). This can include parts of a plant such as buds or fruits or even dead leaves. Some animals feed only upon dead plants and animals.

DEAD LEAVES ————▶ WOODLOUSE ————▶ BLACKBIRD

You are also part of some food chains. Think of some of the things that you eat. Here is one example of a food chain that might involve you:

GRASS ————▶ SHEEP ————▶ HUMAN

▶ Write down some other food chains that include you.
Use arrows to show which way the energy is going.

▶ Look at the woodland picture at the beginning of this topic (page 123).
See how many food chains you can find. Write them down.
Use the arrows to show the direction of the energy flow.

Looking at animals in leaf litter

Put some leaf litter into a white tray.

Carefully sort through it and collect any small animals that you find. You can pick them up with a fine paint brush or by using a pooter.

Be careful that you don't damage them.

Your teacher will give you a sheet showing what each animal eats.

Try to write down possible food chains for the leaf litter.

Wash your hands after this activity.

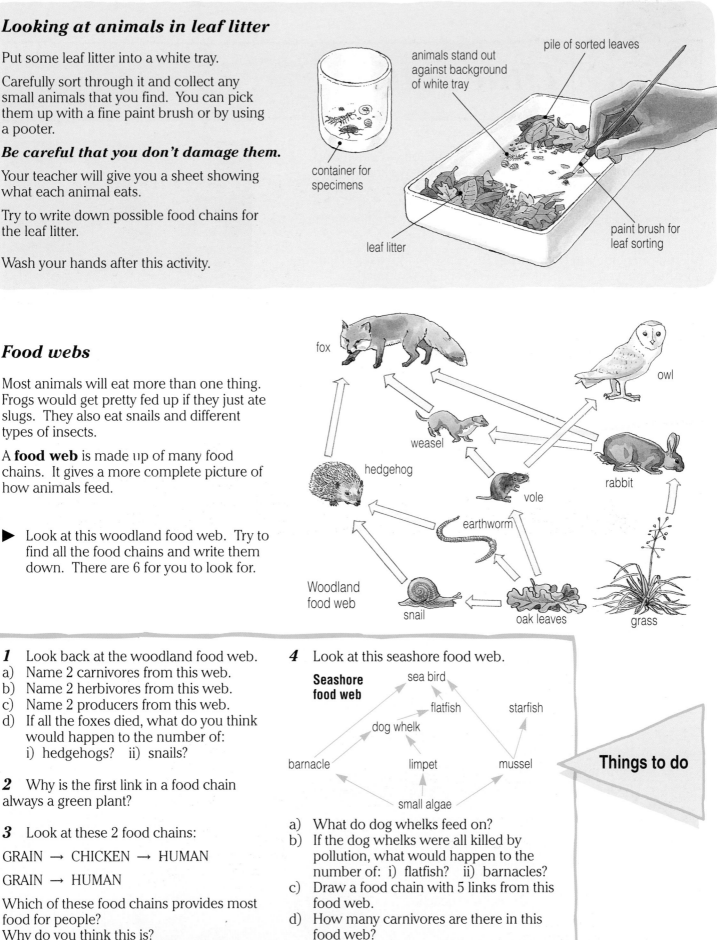

animals stand out against background of white tray

pile of sorted leaves

container for specimens

leaf litter

paint brush for leaf sorting

Food webs

Most animals will eat more than one thing. Frogs would get pretty fed up if they just ate slugs. They also eat snails and different types of insects.

A **food web** is made up of many food chains. It gives a more complete picture of how animals feed.

▶ Look at this woodland food web. Try to find all the food chains and write them down. There are 6 for you to look for.

fox

owl

weasel

hedgehog

vole

rabbit

earthworm

Woodland food web

snail

oak leaves

grass

---

1 Look back at the woodland food web.
a) Name 2 carnivores from this web.
b) Name 2 herbivores from this web.
c) Name 2 producers from this web.
d) If all the foxes died, what do you think would happen to the number of:
i) hedgehogs? ii) snails?

2 Why is the first link in a food chain always a green plant?

3 Look at these 2 food chains:

GRAIN → CHICKEN → HUMAN

GRAIN → HUMAN

Which of these food chains provides most food for people?
Why do you think this is?

4 Look at this seashore food web.

Seashore food web

sea bird

flatfish

starfish

dog whelk

barnacle

limpet

mussel

small algae

a) What do dog whelks feed on?
b) If the dog whelks were all killed by pollution, what would happen to the number of: i) flatfish? ii) barnacles?
c) Draw a food chain with 5 links from this food web.
d) How many carnivores are there in this food web?

Things to do

Little rotters

Look at this photograph of food that has gone off. In olden days people did not know why food went bad. Now we know that **microbes** are to blame.

Microbes are all around us. They are in the air we breathe, in the soil and in untreated water.

Microbes include **bacteria**, **fungi** (moulds) and **viruses**. Many are so small that you need a microscope to see them properly.

Mould growing on some nectarines

Looking at moulds

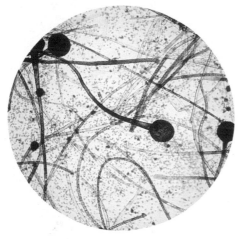

Bread mould under the microscope

Using tweezers place a small piece of bread mould on to a slide.

Add a drop of water and gently lower a cover slip on to the mould. If it does not lie flat, gently tap the cover slip with the end of your tweezers.

▶ Look at the bread mould under your microscope. Describe exactly what you see.

Picking some mould off old bread with tweezers

Lowering cover slip onto mould on a slide

Mouldy bread!

What affects the growth of microbes**?**

Old bread often goes mouldy.
How could you find out what affects how quickly bread goes mouldy**?**

Plan an investigation.

How would you make it a fair test**?**
Decide how you would record your results.
Can you predict any patterns that your results might have**?**

▶ Which conditions do you think ***stop*** the following foods from going bad**?**

a frozen sweetcorn. **d** canned peaches.

b dried peas. **e** packet of crisps.

c vacuum-packed bacon.

Something in the air?

It is now known that microbes make food go bad, but how do they reach the food in the first place?

In this experiment you are going to use **nutrient broth** to grow microbes.

In order to make it a fair test the broth must be **sterilised**. This means that any microbes already present will be killed.

Take 4 test-tubes and pour in nutrient broth to fill each to about a third full.

Set them up as shown in this diagram.

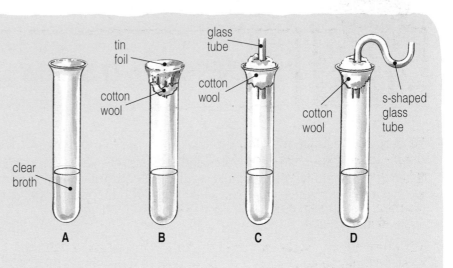

Get your teacher to heat tubes A, B, C and D to a high temperature in a pressure cooker for 15 minutes.

What do you think this will do to the nutrient broth?

Label your test-tubes. Place them in a beaker and leave them at room temperature for one week.

Copy out the table so that you are ready to record your results.

If microbes are present they will turn the broth cloudy.

f In which test-tubes did the broth turn cloudy?

g How did the microbes get to the broth in these tubes?

h Do you think microbes are lighter or heavier than air? Give your reason.

i Why did microbes not get into the broth in test-tube D?

Tube	A	B	C	D
Clear or cloudy?				

Things to do

1 The Cook family went away on their summer holiday for 3 weeks. They left some food out in the kitchen in their hurry to leave.
What do you think will have happened to each of the following foods by the time they return?

> packet of cornflakes   open bottle of milk
> bowl of sugar   jar of jam (with lid off)
> piece of cheese   tin of grapefruit
> apple   packet of salted peanuts
> bowl of cat meat

2 Find out about 3 microbes that are harmful to people and 3 microbes that are useful.

3 Many food packets have 'sell by' or 'use by' dates on them.
Make a list of some of the foods that are marked with these dates.
What do you think might happen to the food after this date?
Canned and dried foods don't need a 'sell by' date. Why is this?

4 Louis Pasteur was a French scientist famous for his work on microbes. Find out about his work.

Ashes to ashes

We have already seen that microbes can make food go rotten.
Microbes can also make dead plants and animals rot.
Instead of saying they rot, we could say they **decompose**.
We call microbes which can make dead things rot **decomposers**.
They can digest dead things just as we digest our food.

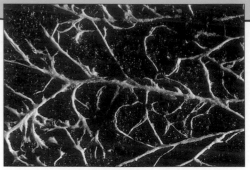
Fungus growing on compost

Heaps of microbes!

Have you seen a **compost heap** in a garden?
This is a place where dead plant material is put. Microbes grow
well here and rot down the plant material to form a compost.
Gardeners dig the compost into the soil to improve it for growing
plants.

▶ Look at this diagram of a compost heap.

a Why do you think the heap has holes in the sides and base?

b Why do you think the heap has a lid?

c The heap is sometimes turned with a fork. Why is this?

d It is important that the heap is kept moist but not soaking.
Why do you think this is?

e The heap rots quicker in summer than in winter. Why is this?

f What conditions do you think are needed for decay by microbes
to occur?

A compost heap

A lot of rot or not?

Things that rot are **biodegradable**.

Materials that never rot are **non-biodegradable**.

▶ Look at this photograph.

g Which of the items shown do you think are biodegradable?

h Why do non-biodegradable materials cause problems for
our environment?

▶ How do you think the following non-biodegradable items
might harm wildlife?

i Broken glass on a path.

j A milk bottle in a hedge.

k Angler's lead weights in a pond.

l Lost plastic fishing nets in the sea.

Finding out which microbes rot grass

Take 3 petri-dishes containing sterile agar jelly. The jelly is a food for microbes.

Label your dishes A, B and C.

Using sterile tweezers add some boiled grass to dish A,
add some freshly cut grass to dish B,
leave dish C unopened.

Use sticky tape to fix the lid of each dish to its base.

Place them in an incubator at 25 °C and leave them for a few days.

After a few days look for any sign that microbes are present.
Do not open the dishes.

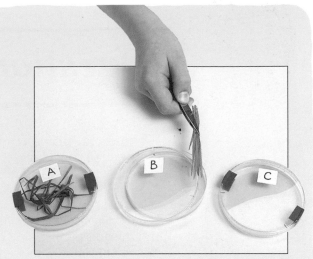

m Why was the grass in dish A boiled first?

n Why was dish C left unopened?

o Why were the dishes kept at 25 °C?

Dig this!

You can find out which things are biodegradable just by burying them in the soil. If you dig them up at different times afterwards you can see if they are rotting.

Plan an investigation to see which things rot and how fast they rot.

What sort of things would you use?
Your teacher can help you with some suggestions.

How often would you dig up and examine the things that you bury?

How could you measure and record how much of anything had rotted?

Can you predict any patterns that your results might have?

---

1 Sometimes dead things do not decompose. Say why you think each of the following did not rot.

a) In Siberia the bodies of animals called mammoths have been found in frozen ground. They are thousands of years old.

b) Human bodies (hundreds of years old) have been found in acid peat bogs.

c) The ancient Egyptians buried their kings as mummies. This involved drying out the body in a burial chamber to preserve it.

2 The hard parts of animals sometimes do not decay. They may be preserved as fossils. Find out how this can take place and write a brief report.

3 A farmer wants to preserve grass to feed her animals in the winter. She can do this in two ways. Either she can pack it tightly in a large container so that air cannot get in (this makes silage), or she can dry the grass out to make hay.
Explain why:
a) silage, and
b) hay
do not rot.

Things to do

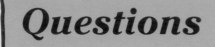

Questions

1 Choose: a) an insect b) a bird and c) a mammal.
For each of your choices, say where it lives (its habitat), what it feeds on and how it is adapted to its habitat.

2 George says: "when I dig my compost, steam comes out of it".
Plan an investigation to find out how much heat is given off by rotting grass.
You can use the sort of equipment found in your science laboratory.
Remember to make your investigation a fair test. Do not try out your plan unless you have checked it with your teacher.

3 See if you can make a food chain out of these:
a) thrush, cabbage, caterpillar
b) slug, hedgehog, lettuce
c) tiny plants, fish, water fleas, tadpoles
d) greenfly, blackbird, ladybird, rose bush.

4 Look at the 3 temperature graphs below.
a) See if you can match them up with London, Singapore and Alaska.
b) Give a reason for your choice in each case.
c) Which of these places do you think would be the most difficult for plants and animals to survive in? Give your reasons.

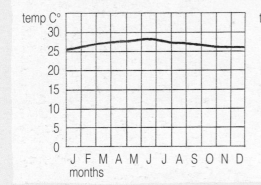
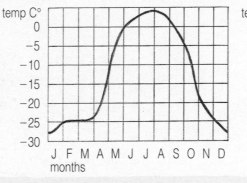
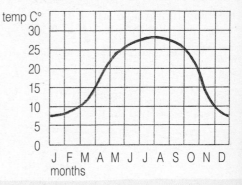

5 I am a microbe. I really like rotting things down.
I live in Mouldy Manor, which has just been deserted by its owners.
Write about my decaying adventures.

6 Some pupils did a survey of a small woodland habitat. They identified and counted all the trees. The table shows their results.
a) Draw a bar-chart of these results.
b) Which were the 2 most common trees in the wood?

Name of tree	Number in wood
ash	8
beech	15
birch	20
holly	2
oak	4

7 Milk can be preserved in a number of ways:
a) pasteurised b) sterilised c) ultra-high temperature (UHT).
Find out about each of these methods.
Why does pasteurised milk turn sour even in a sealed bottle?
Why do sterilised and UHT milk keep so long in their containers?

Rocks

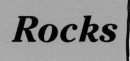

Have you ever seen a volcano?
When it erupts, red hot lava pours out of the cone.
When the lava cools it forms rock.
But this is only one way of forming rock.
In this topic you will find out about other ways.

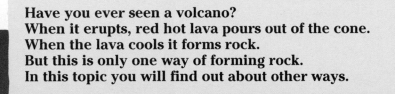

In this topic:

11a *Rock groups*
11b *Looking at weathering*
11c *Erosion*
11d *Settling down*
11e *Rocks over time*

Rock groups

Rocks are found in many different shapes and sizes.
Maybe you have climbed some of the larger ones ...
or maybe you have collected some.

Rocks can tell us a lot about the history of our planet, Earth.

People who study rocks are called **geologists**.
Let's see how good a geologist you can be!

Testing rocks

Carry out these tests on each rock sample.

Your teacher will give you some Rock Data Cards.
Write down the results for each rock on a new Rock Data Card.

Rock test 1 – What does the rock look like?

Use a magnifying glass to observe the rock carefully.
- What colour is it?
- Is it rough or smooth?
- Is it shiny or dull?
- Can you see any crystals or grains?

Rock test 2 – Is the rock hard?

Try to scratch the rock.
Rocks which can be scratched by a fingernail are called **very soft**.
Rocks which can be scratched by an iron nail are called **soft**.
Rocks which can be scratched by a steel knife are called **hard**.
Rocks which cannot be scratched by a steel knife are called **very hard**.

Rock test 3 – Does the rock break easily?

Wrap the sample in a cloth. Put it on the floor.
Lower your heel onto the rock. Push down.
Does the rock break?

Rock test 4 – Does the rock soak up water?

Put the sample on a watch glass.
Use a pipette to drop water on to it.
What happens to the water?

Look at your Rock Data Cards. Study the properties of the samples.

Now divide the rocks into groups. List your groups.

Write down the properties you have used to make groups.

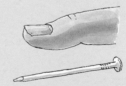

Rock data card
Sample number
Rock test 1

Rock test 2

Rock test 3

Rock test 4

Other information

Rocks contain different particles or grains.
Some grains fit together well.
But in some rocks the grains do not fit so well.

Think about the rocks which soak up water.
Where do you think the water goes?
What does this tell you about how the grains fit together?

Measure how much water a rock soaks up

Another way of grouping rocks is by the way they were made.

There are 3 main types of rock.
The 3 types were formed in different ways.

Granite (igneous)

Igneous rocks
These form when melted ('molten')
substances cool.
These rocks are usually hard.
They are made of crystals.
Granite is an igneous rock.

Sedimentary rocks
These form in layers. They are made
when substances settle out in water.
Sometimes they contain fossils.
These rocks are usually soft.
Sandstone and **limestone** are
sedimentary rocks.

Sandstone (sedimentary)

Metamorphic rocks
These rocks form much more slowly.
They are made when rocks are heated
and pushed together.
They are usually very hard.
Marble is a metamorphic rock formed
from limestone.

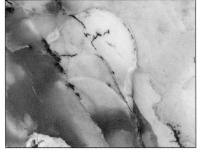
Marble (metamorphic)

Limestone (sedimentary)

1 Copy and complete the following:
a) There are 3 main types of rock: . . . . ,
. . . . and . . . .
b) . . . . rocks form when hot liquids cool
and become solid.
c) . . . . rocks form as substances settle in
layers.
d) . . . . rocks form when other rocks are
heated and pushed together.

2 Use your rock test findings, books and
computer to decide whether your rock
samples were igneous, sedimentary or
metamorphic.

3 Some types of rock are used in buildings.
a) What are the ideal properties of a rock
used for building?
b) Find out what types of rock are used for
your local buildings.
Draw a poster
about this to
display in your
local library.

Things to do

4 Can you explain
how the rocks in this
photograph have
changed?

Looking at weathering

Rocks don't stay the same forever.
They slowly crumble away.

▶ Look at these photographs and say what you think has caused
the rocks to change in each case.

The process that makes rocks crumble is called **weathering**.
Weathering can be caused by water, wind and changes of
temperature.

Acid attack

Do you remember looking at how acid rainwater affected limestone
in Topic 6?

Carry out an investigation to see if acid affects other rocks in the
same way.

Add a few drops of acid to chalk.

Write down what you see.

⚠️ acid

acid

Repeat your investigation with granite, sandstone and marble chips.

Frost damage

Water can get into cracks in rocks.

If the water freezes, it turns to ice. But ice takes up more space than
water. So the ice can split the rock into smaller pieces. This is
called frost damage.

Your teacher will fill a small glass bottle with water and
screw the top on tightly.

The bottle is then put into a strong plastic bag, which is
tied and put into a freezer.

In the next lesson your teacher will show you what has
happened to the bottle.

This limestone cave was weathered out by water.

Large **stalactites** hang from the roof of the cave.

How do you think they formed?

Investigating weathering

Look at rocks around your school for signs of weathering. You can also look at bricks and other building materials.

- Are the weathered rocks soft?
  Scratch them with an iron nail to find out.

- What colour are they?
  Is their colour different from that of unchanged rock?

- Are there any cracks in their surface? What are the cracks like?

- What do you think caused the weathering in each case?

- What types of rock crumble most easily?

- What types of rock last the longest?

Look to see how mosses, lichens and other plants can change rocks. Examine the rock underneath these plants and then carefully replace them.

▶ Find out about different types of weathering:
  - physical weathering
  - chemical weathering
  - biological weathering.

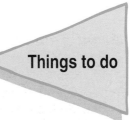

Things to do

1 Copy and complete the following: The process that makes rocks crumble is called . . . . Soft rocks crumble more easily than . . . . rocks. Rocks break up due to the action of . . . . , ... or . . . . Rain can weather rocks because it is . . . . When water gets into cracks it can . . . . to form . . . . which takes up more space and so it can split the rock into smaller pieces.

2 Look at this diagram. Write an explanation of how loose scree forms.

loose scree

3 Visit your nearest churchyard or cemetery. But never go on your own. Always take a friend or an adult with you. Look carefully at the different types of gravestone. Some will have weathered more than others. What are the earliest dates that you can read? These will be on the hardest rocks. Try to name the different types of rock and note the earliest date on each.

11c *Erosion*

Weathering makes rocks crumble into smaller pieces.

These pieces are then carried away by other things, e.g. wind, and so the rock wears away.

This wearing away of rocks is called **erosion**.

CRUMBLE COTTAGE
LAND-SLIDE WRECKS CLIFF HOMES

The Robinsons are moving house, because their house is on the move.
The garden is not what it was, in fact it's nearly all gone.

The floors are tilting and the walls are cracking.
The Robinsons, who have lived there for 30 years, said 'We are so sad. When we

bought the house we never thought that this would happen.'

► Study the newspaper article above and then write down your answers to these questions.

a Why do you think the Robinsons bought a house so close to the cliff edge?

b What do you think caused the land-slide?

c Is there any way it could have been prevented?

d What do you think has happened to all the bits of rock that have been eroded from the cliff?

► Look at these 3 photographs. For each one, write down what you think is causing the erosion of the rocks.

e

f

g

<table>
<tr><td>

Weathering
The rocks break into pieces.

</td><td>

Erosion
The small pieces of rock rub against others as they move. They get smaller themselves and they wear away other rocks as they move along.

</td></tr>
</table>

The pieces of rock are often found a long way from where they started.
Rock pieces are transported by rivers.

How are rocks eroded by water?

Make a 'stream' flowing into a 'lake'.
Investigate how the stream moves rocks.
Is the movement affected by:

- how fast the stream flows?
- the width of the stream?
- the type of rock?
- the size of rock?

Make a prediction which you could test.

Write a plan to test your prediction.

How can you make your results reliable?

Show your plan to your teacher and then try it out.

Write a report saying what you did and what you found out.

Was your plan a good one?

How could you improve your investigation?

Solve the mystery

▶ Look at these 2 photographs.
Write down your answers to these questions.

h How do you think erosion has formed the **arch** and the **stacks?**

i Where has the material that was eroded ended up?

1 Copy and complete, choosing the correct word from the 2 given in brackets in each case:
Rocks crumble due to (weathering/erosion) and are then worn away by (weathering/erosion). (Winds/waves) break off pieces of rock when they smash against (hills/cliffs). Glaciers are rivers of (ice/water) that scrape rock out of (mountains/valleys). (Larger/smaller) pieces of rock are carried further away than (larger/smaller) pieces.

2 Design a model to show how waves erode cliffs.
What will you make the cliffs out of?
How will you make the waves hit the cliffs?

3 In very dry countries, winds can pick up sand and blow it against large rocks.
Look at this photograph of a **rock pedestal**.
Try to explain how these are formed in the desert.

4 Ask your teacher for some pebbles from a beach. What sort of shapes do they have? How do you think they have become shaped like this?

Things to do

Settling down

After rocks are broken down, the smaller pieces may be carried away. We say that they are **transported** to another place.

▶ In what ways can the pieces be transported to another place? Look back at page 140 for some ideas.

Eventually the pieces of rock are **deposited** in another area.
Very small pieces of rock are called **sediments**.
Sediments deposited by the sea may form sand banks.
When a river deposits sediments, they may eventually form a soil.

Near a sandy bay

Where does the soil come from?

▶ Your teacher will give you samples of
4 different soils.
These will be labelled A, B, C and D.
Each of these soils has come from a
different place.

Look very carefully at each soil using
a hand lens.
Try to match each soil with one of the
places shown in these photographs.
Write down the reasons for your choice.

Moorland

Farmland

Woodland

It's a fact!

Sandy soils have large particles and clay soils have small particles. **Loam soils** are a mixture of sandy soil and clay soil. They are easy to dig and hold water without becoming water-logged.
Dead plants and animals decay in soil to form a soft black substance called **humus**.

Investigating soils

Your teacher will give you 2 different soil samples.
You can choose one of these investigations:

> **A** Which soil contains more water?

> **C** Which soil will hold the most water?

> **B** Which soil contains more humus?
> (Hint: humus burns off at 110°C.)

> **D** In which soil do seeds grow better?

Plan your investigation. Make sure it is a fair test.

- What equipment will you need?
- How will you record your results?

Looking at sediments

▶ Look very carefully at your rock and soil sample with a hand lens.
Are all the particles the same size?

▶ Pour some of your material into a jam jar or measuring cylinder.
There should be enough to fill the measuring cylinder to a depth
of about 4 cm.

Now almost fill the container with water. Put your hand over
the top and carefully shake the container, so that you mix the
solid up with the water.

Leave the solid to settle.
Look at it regularly during the lesson.

Write down what you can see.

Have another look at it next lesson.

What does this experiment tell you about sediments?

1 Copy and complete:
Soils are made of small . . . . particles. These
have broken away from large rocks by . . . .
and . . . . Then they may have been . . . . by
the action of rivers and streams. Sediments
are small . . . . particles. Some may have
been . . . . by the sea to form sand.

2 Try to explain each of the following
statements:
a) Sandy soils are easy to dig but need
plenty of rain.
b) Clay soils can get water-logged and are
then hard to dig.

3 The rock cycle:

> Rocks can be broken down by
> weathering and erosion. They can then
> be transported and deposited
> somewhere else. When they build up
> as sediments they become squashed
> together to form a new rock.

Make a poster or patterned note of the
rock cycle.

4 Estuaries are places where rivers meet
the sea. The sediment carried by the river is
deposited as mud. Find out about estuaries
and mud-flats.

Things to do

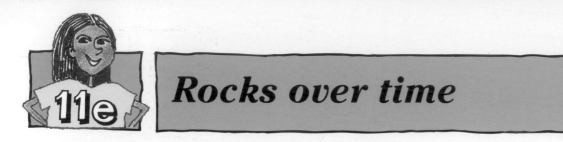

Rocks over time

▶ Read again about igneous, sedimentary and metamorphic rocks on page 137.
Now look back to page 143.
How do you think sedimentary rocks form?

Sedimentary rocks

You know that rocks are weathered.
The small pieces of rock are carried to another place.
They then **deposit** as **sediment**.

Over time layers of sediment pile up.
This puts pressure on older layers underneath.
Water is squeezed out of the sediments.
The pressure pushes the layers of sediment together.
A **sedimentary** rock slowly forms.

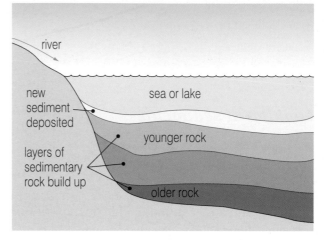

Layers of sedimentary rock forming

At certain times the sea or lake may run dry.

a How could this happen?

This could cause another sediment. Another layer could form.
Try the experiment to see how.

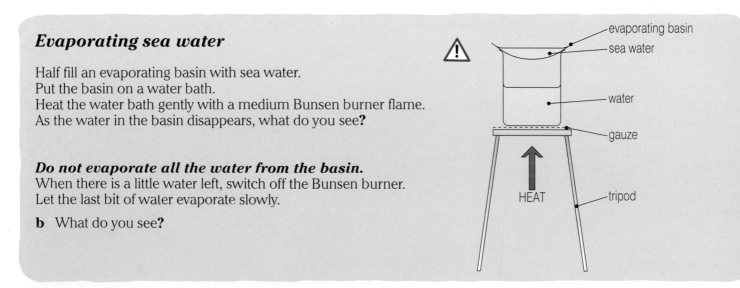

Evaporating sea water

Half fill an evaporating basin with sea water.
Put the basin on a water bath.
Heat the water bath gently with a medium Bunsen burner flame.
As the water in the basin disappears, what do you see?

Do not evaporate all the water from the basin.
When there is a little water left, switch off the Bunsen burner.
Let the last bit of water evaporate slowly.

b What do you see?

Looking at layers of rock tells us about the climate of the Earth millions of years ago.

Rocks that tell a story

Rocks give us evidence that the Earth is
very old ... about 4600 million years old!

Fossils tell us about the animals and plants that lived
millions of years ago. They are the remains of animals and plants
that have been preserved in rocks.

▶ Look at the fossil your group has been given.

How do you think this fossil formed**?**

Use books or ROMs to find out about your fossil.
- When did it live**?**
- Where did it live**?**
- What was its environment like**?**

Write a paragraph about your fossil.

Draw a picture of your fossil and colour it in.

▶ Look at the time chart below. This chart shows
4600 million years of the Earth's history.

Where does your *fossil* fit on the time chart**?**

Where are *you* on the time chart**?**

c Are fossils young or old compared to you**?**

d Are fossils young or old compared to the Earth**?**

Earth begins   4000 million years   3000 million years   2000 million years   1000 million years   now

---

1 Rocks can be broken down into smaller
pieces.
This is called . . . . The small pieces are . . . .
to another place. They can wear away more
rock. This is called . . . .
The rocks deposit. Layers of . . . . build up.
The . . . . pushes the sediment layers
together.
A . . . . rock forms.
When water . . . . from seas and . . . ., this
also leaves sediments which form layers in
the rock.

2 Write down your answers to these
questions.
a) What are fossils?
b) Why is it rare to find fossils in
metamorphic rocks?

3 Describe the changes in how a rock
looks as it is transported further and further.

4 Find out about more plants and animals
that lived long ago. Put the names of these
onto your time chart in the correct places.

Things to do

Questions

1 Say whether each of the following statements is *true* or *false*.
a) Sedimentary rocks are usually very hard.
b) Igneous rocks form when molten materials cool.
c) Rocks are often found on beaches.
d) Sandstone is a sedimentary rock.
e) There are 2 main types of rock.

2 Draw pictures of some of the rock samples you tested.
Cut out the pictures.
Stick them on to the backs of your Rock Data Cards.

3 Use reference books or ROMs to find
out how coal forms.
Write a paragraph and draw diagrams
to explain this process.

4 Where can you find rock samples?
In what sort of places?
Collecting rock samples can be dangerous.

Imagine you are the teacher of a class.
The class is going to search for rock
samples.
You want to make sure the rocks will
be collected safely.
Write down some instructions for your
class.
Make sure you give safety guidelines.

5 Sedimentary rocks take a long time to
form. The sediments settle in water.
Design an investigation to see how quickly
different sediments settle.
Sediments to test could be:
soil, sand, pebbles, silt.

6 Wackham Wanderers are fed up with their soccer pitch.
At the start of the season it's bone dry and full of cracks.
For most of the rest of the season it's water-logged.
a) Plan an investigation to find out how well the water in the soil
drains away.
You can use the sort of equipment found in your science
laboratory. Remember to make it a fair test.
b) Suggest ways in which the Wanderers could improve
the drainage of their pitch.

Sight and Sound

Our eyes and our ears help us to make sense of the world around us. And they help us to learn about science.

Our eyes use light energy, and our ears use sound energy.

Together they let us recognise friends and warn us of danger.

▶ Close your eyes and think what it would be like to be completely blind.
Write down 3 things that you could not do if you were blind.

▶ Hold a mirror in front of you, and look at your eye. You are looking at an **image** of your eye.
The coloured part of your eye is called the **iris**.
Make an accurate drawing of your iris.

The dark hole in the middle of your iris is called the **pupil**. This lets the light enter your eye.

▶ Keep looking in the mirror while you turn your head to point to a dark part of the room and then to a bright window.
Look carefully.
What happens to the size of your pupil?
Why is this?

▶ Look at this diagram of your eye:
Study the different parts of it.

▶ Your teacher will give you a copy of this diagram. Fill in the missing words on the sheet.

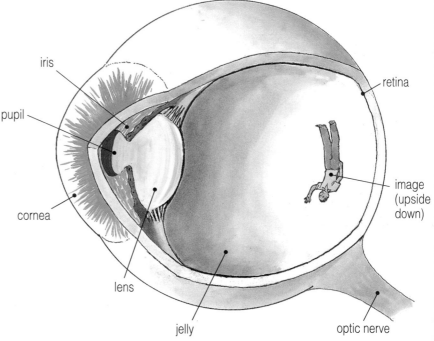

iris — retina — pupil — cornea — lens — jelly — image (upside down) — optic nerve

How do you see?

Emma has a hypothesis about how she can see things:

Tina has a different hypothesis:

- Which hypothesis do you think is correct?

- Write some sentences to explain your reasons.
Try to use these words:

  light   reflected   eye   pupil

- Can you think of an investigation that will decide between these two hypotheses?

Emma says: "I think the light always has to travel to my eye and then to the book so that I can see it."

Tina says: "I think the light always has to travel to the book and then be reflected up into my eye."

Are two eyes better than one?

- Do you think you can judge distances better with one eye or two? Write down your prediction.

- Plan a short investigation to test this.
  You can use a quick test of skill such as:
  hold out a pencil in each hand at arm's length and try to make the pencil points touch each other.

- Do your investigation. What do you find?

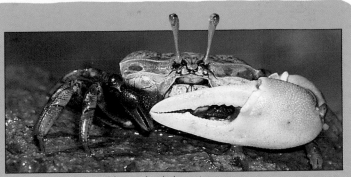
Most animals have two eyes

Shadows

▶ Shine a torch or a **ray-box** at a white sheet of paper.
  Hold an object so that you see a **shadow** on the screen.

a Why is the screen bright?

b Why is the shadow dark?

c How can you make the shadow larger?

light rays

light bulb

ray box

screen

The light travels in straight lines. So we can draw straight lines called **rays** to show where the light is going.

d How can you use your ruler to check that the light rays travel in straight lines?

---

1 Copy and complete:
When I look at this page, the . . . . rays are reflected off the white paper and then travel into my . . . . The rays make an . . . . on my retina. In a dim light my pupil grows . . . . so that more . . . . can get into my . . . .

2 In a thunderstorm you see the lightning and then hear the thunder.
What does this tell you about the speed of light?

3 Draw a design for a clock that uses shadows from the Sun.

4 Get a piece of card about 10 cm x 10 cm. On one side draw a bird (using thick lines). On the other side draw a cage. Tape a pencil to the card so that you can spin it quickly between your hands. What do you see?
Write a sentence to explain what you think is happening. Then design a different card.

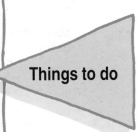
Things to do

Mirrors and reflections

Light rays can be *reflected*.

You can see this page because light rays are being reflected off the white paper and into your eyes.

Where the light shines on this black ink, it is not reflected – it is **absorbed**.

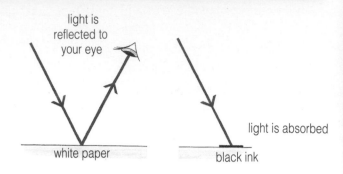

A mirror is a good reflector of light.
When you look in a mirror, you see an **image** of yourself.

▶ Think about all the ways that mirrors are used – in homes, shops and cars. Make a list of all the uses you can think of.

How can you use a mirror on a sunny day to send a message to a distant friend?

If your bedroom is dark, how can you use a mirror to make it look brighter?

A flat mirror is called a **plane** mirror.
Here is an experiment to see what happens when light is reflected off a plane mirror.

The Law of Reflection

Your teacher will give you a Help Sheet with some lines and angles marked on it.

1 Set your plane mirror with its **back** along the line marked 'mirror' (the light is reflected from the silver back of the mirror).

2 Use a ray-box to send a narrow beam of light (a 'ray') along the line marked 20° on the **angle of incidence** scale.

3 Measure the **angle of reflection**. What do you find?

4 Repeat this using different angles of incidence.

5 Write down your conclusion.

• If the angle of incidence was 34°, what do you think the angle of reflection would be? Predict it and then try it.

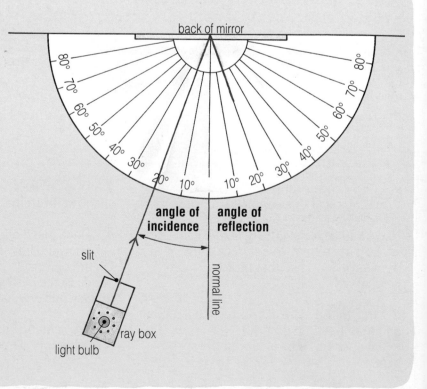

Mirror images

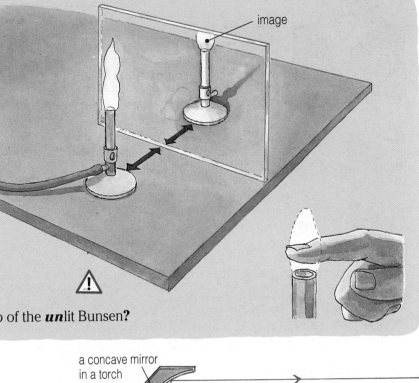

1 Fix a sheet of glass so that it is upright on the table.

2 Put a Bunsen burner with a bright yellow flame in front of it.

3 Look into the 'mirror' to see the image of the flame. Where does it appear to be?

4 Move another **un**lit Bunsen burner until the image of the flame sits exactly on it.

5 Measure the distances of the two Bunsen burners from the glass mirror. What do you find?

6 Try this using different distances.

7 Write down your conclusion.

- What do you see if you put your finger on top of the **un**lit Bunsen?

Curved mirrors

Curved mirrors can be **convex** (like the back of a spoon) or **concave** (like the front of a spoon).

A **concave** mirror is used in a torch and in a car headlight:

a concave mirror in a torch · light rays · light bulb

A **concave** mirror is also used in a solar cooker:

This is a cheap source of energy in some countries.

sun's rays · pan or kettle · concave mirror used for cooking

---

1 Look at this notice:

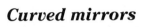

The Law of Reflection
The angle of incidence is **equal** to the angle of reflection

a) How can you read it easily?
b) Copy it out correctly.
c) Copy and complete:
The distance from an object to a plane mirror is . . . . to the distance from the . . . . to the mirror.

2 Write your name so that it reads correctly when viewed in a mirror.

3 Where and why might you see:

AMBULANCE

4 Imagine you wake up tomorrow in a world where light is never reflected. Write a story about it.

5 Read the next two pages (Unit 12c) and decide what you need to bring to the next lesson.

Things to do

Using light rays

▶ Choose either • the **pin-hole camera** (below)
   or • the **periscope** (opposite page)
and then build it.

Making a pin-hole camera

▶ Look at the diagrams and then decide
how to make your camera.

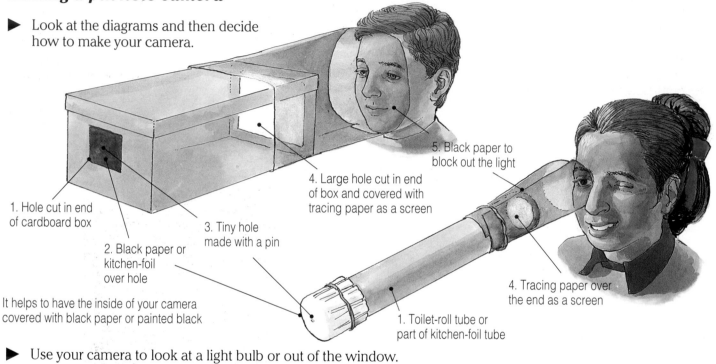

1. Hole cut in end
of cardboard box

2. Black paper or
kitchen-foil
over hole

3. Tiny hole
made with a pin

4. Large hole cut in end
of box and covered with
tracing paper as a screen

5. Black paper to
block out the light

It helps to have the inside of your camera
covered with black paper or painted black

4. Tracing paper over
the end as a screen

1. Toilet-roll tube or
part of kitchen-foil tube

▶ Use your camera to look at a light bulb or out of the window.

a What do you see?

b Which way up is the **image**? (We say it is **inverted**.)
Can you explain why?
(Hint: think of the light rays coming in through the hole.)

c How could this camera be used by an artist to make a painting?

d If you wanted to take a photo, where would you put the film?

e What happens if you make the pin-hole wider? Try it.
Is the image brighter or darker? Why?
Is the image sharper or more blurred? Why?

f Explain how your camera works, using the words:

> **light rays**   **pin-hole**   **straight lines**   **image**

g How could you make the image twice as big?

• If you have time, make the pin-hole much bigger and then
put a lens over the hole. Move the lens until you get a sharp
and bright image. You have made a lens camera.

A photo taken with a pin-hole camera.

Making a periscope

▶ Look at these diagrams and then make your own periscope.

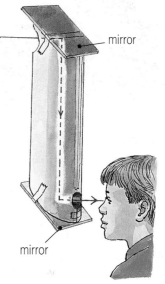
mirror

mirror

1. Roll of cardboard (or the tube from the centre of a kitchen-foil roll, or the box it is sold in, or two/three toilet-roll tubes).

2. Cut off the ends, at exactly 45°, as shown.

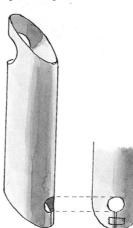

3. Make two viewing holes as shown.

Cut the card, then sellotape afterwards.

The bottom hole can be small but make the top one as big as you can.

4. Put the mirrors in place and hold them with sellotape.

Adjust the mirrors – and the viewing holes – until you can see through your periscope properly.

▶ Use your periscope to look over an object (the table or the window-sill).

h What do you see?
You are looking at an ***image*** in the mirrors.

i Describe the image that you see. For example:
- Is it the same way up as the real thing?
- Is it the same size as the real thing?
- Is it the same colour as the real thing?

j How can you use your periscope to see round a corner?

k How many different uses for a periscope can you think of? Make a list.

l How could you change the design so that you could see backwards over your head? Sketch a design for this.

m Explain how your periscope works, using the words:

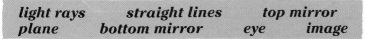

| *light rays* | *straight lines* | *top mirror* |
| *plane* | *bottom mirror* | *eye*   *image* |

---

1 Copy and complete:
In a pin-hole . . . . , the light . . . . enter through the . . . . and travel in . . . . lines to the screen where they form an . . . .
The image is . . . . (upside-down).
If the pin-hole is made . . . . , the image is brighter but more blurred.

2 Explain how you can convert a pin-hole camera into a lens camera. What is the advantage of doing this?

3 Copy and complete:
In a periscope, the light . . . . enter the top hole and are . . . . by the top mirror, so that they travel . . . . the tube to the bottom . . . . , where they are . . . . into your . . . . , so that you see an . . . .

4 A driver is using her car to pull a caravan, but it blocks her view through the driving mirror.
Design a periscope to solve the problem, and draw a labelled sketch.

Things to do

Sound moves

▶ Sit quietly and just *listen*. Make a list of all the sounds you can hear in one minute.

▶ Write down as many 'sound' words as you can. For example, boom, bang, crash, squeak, . . .

▶ Touch the front of your throat while you make an 'aaah' sound. Can you feel it *vibrating*?

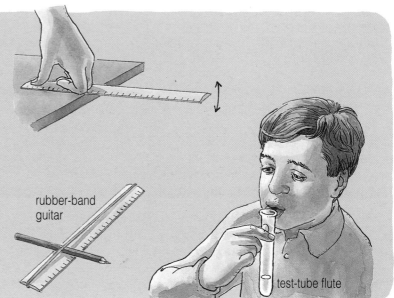

Hold a ruler firmly with part of it over the edge of the table. Then twang it.

a What is the end of the ruler doing?

b When does it stop making a sound?

c How can you make the sound quieter? How can you make it louder?

d How can you make it sound a higher note? And then a lower note? Can you play a tune – for example, 'Jingle Bells'?

Now repeat steps **a** to **d** with the other two 'musical instruments' shown here:

What do you find? Can you see any patterns? Write down your conclusions.

rubber-band guitar

test-tube flute

To make the ruler vibrate, you had to give it some *energy*.

e Where did this energy come from?

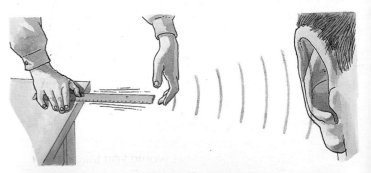

The vibrating ruler sends out sound waves through the air. Some of this sound energy travels to your ear, and so you can hear the sound.

Sound can travel a long way. In a thunderstorm, you can see a flash of lightning and then later you can hear the sound of it (the thunder).

f Which travels faster, light or sound?

Sound travels about 330 metres in one second. (Light travels almost a million times faster, at 300 000 000 metres per second.)

g How far would sound travel in 2 seconds?

h If you hear thunder 10 seconds after the lightning flash, how far away is the storm?

Echoes

If you clap your hands in front of a big building, you may hear an **echo**.

This happens because the sound wave is ***reflected*** back to you. The building is like a mirror.

Suppose you heard the echo after 2 seconds.

i How long did it take for the sound to get ***to the wall?***

j How far away is the wall, if the speed of sound is 330 metres per second**?**

sound wave travels to the wall

clap

and back again

Echo-sounding

Sailors can use echoes to find the depth of the sea, using an ***echo-sounder*** or ***sonar***.

Suppose this ship sent out a sound wave, and it got back an echo after 1 second.

k How long did it take the sound to get to the bottom of the sea**?**

Sound travels faster in water. It travels at 1500 metres per second.

l How far will the sound travel in $\frac{1}{2}$ second**?**

m How deep is the sea under the ship**?**

n If the shoal of fish in the diagram swims under the boat, how will the captain know**?**

The sound used by the sonar is too high for us to hear. It is called **ultrasonic** sound or **ultrasound**.

Dolphins use ultrasound to find their food. They make high-pitched squeaks and listen to the echoes.

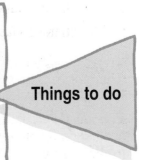

Bats also use ultrasonic sounds, so that they can find food and 'see' in the dark.

▶ Plan an investigation to find the speed of sound.
- What equipment would you need**?**
- What measurements would you take**?**
- How would you calculate the speed**?**

---

1 Copy and complete:
a) All . . . . are caused by vibrations.
b) Echoes are due to the . . . . of sound.
c) The speed of sound is 330 . . . . per second.

2 Think about the noise in your school dining-hall. Write a list of suggestions for making it quieter.

3 Watching a cricket match from a distance, it seems that the bat hits the ball before you hear it. Explain this.

4 Karen hears an echo from a cliff after 4 seconds. How far is she from the cliff?

5 Write a poem using as many 'sound' words as possible.

Things to do

Hear, hear!

▶ Look at this diagram of your ear.
Study the different parts of it.

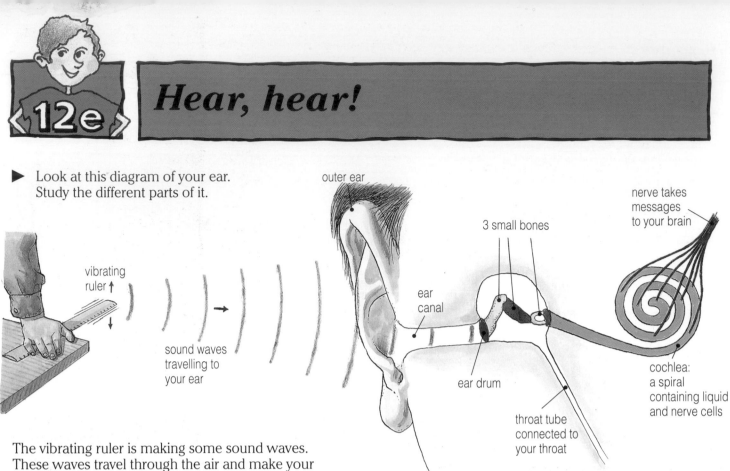

vibrating
ruler ↑
↓

sound waves
travelling to
your ear

outer ear

3 small bones

nerve takes
messages
to your brain

ear
canal

ear drum

throat tube
connected to
your throat

cochlea:
a spiral
containing liquid
and nerve cells

The vibrating ruler is making some sound waves.
These waves travel through the air and make your
ear-drum vibrate.
This makes the 3 small bones vibrate, and they make the liquid in
your **cochlea** vibrate. This affects the nerve cells in the cochlea and
a message is sent to your brain . . . and so you hear the sound.

▶ Your teacher will give you a copy of this diagram.
Fill in the missing words on it.

Looking after your ears

Your ear is very delicate and can easily be damaged.
This damage can cause deafness.

- Your ear canal can become blocked with wax. If
so, the doctor can wash it out.

- Your ear-drum can be torn by a very loud bang, or
damaged by an infection. It may mend itself, or
doctors can graft a new one.

- Your ear bones may stick together and stop
vibrating properly. An operation can fix this.

- Your 'middle ear' (the small bones and the throat
tube) may be infected. Antibiotics can cure this.

- Your cochlea can be damaged by loud noises – for
example, at pop concerts, near noisy machines, or
wearing 'walkman' headphones. There is **no** cure!

As people get older, their ears work less well. Partial
deafness can be helped by wearing a **hearing-aid**. It
amplifies the sound to make it louder.

Wearing 'ear defenders' at work

How does the size of your outer ear affect your hearing?

Investigate whether the size of the outer ear affects how well you can hear faint sounds.

You can make yourself larger 'ears' from card.

- What faint sounds will you try to hear?
- How can you carry out a fair test of different ear sizes?
- How will you record your results?
- How can you make your results more reliable?

Do your investigation. What do you find?

Does the **size** of the ear matter, or the **shape** of the ear, or both?

Sketch the shapes you have used.

Look at this bush-baby.
What conclusions can you make?

Are two ears better than one?

Investigate whether someone can tell the direction of a sound better with two ears or one.

- How will you make sure the person being tested uses only their ears?
- What will you use to make a sound?
- How will you make it a fair test?
- How will you record your results? Can you record them on a diagram or a map?

Show your plan to your teacher and then do it.

What do you find? Which is better: one ear or two?

Are people more accurate in some directions than others?

Write a report explaining what you did and what you found.

1 Someone plucks a guitar string and you hear it. Explain, step by step, what happens between the guitar string and your brain.

2 Design a poster to encourage teenagers to look after their ears better.

3 People sometimes cup their hands behind their ears when they are trying to hear. Explain why this helps, using all these words if you can:

vibrations	sound waves	
	reflection	like a mirror
concave	sound energy	ear

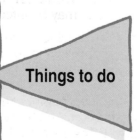

Things to do

1 Design a lighting scheme for your bedroom. Show where you would put the lights, and where you might put some mirrors to make the room brighter.

2 Most animals have two eyes.
'Hunter' animals (like owls) have their eyes at the front of their heads.
'Hunted' animals (like rabbits) have theirs at the side of their heads.
Why do you think this is?

3 Look at your pen. Explain how you are able to see it.

4 Plan an investigation to see if snooker balls (or tennis balls) are reflected off a wall following the same rule as for light rays.
Draw a diagram and explain exactly how you would do it.

5 Can you find 6 consecutive letters in the alphabet that look the same when a mirror is placed to reflect half the letter?
Which other letters are symmetrical?

6 Draw a map of a sharp and dangerous bend in a road.
On the map show where you could place a mirror to make the bend safer for drivers.

7 The diagram shows a side view of a pin-hole camera, with an object in front of it.
Copy the diagram and then draw a ray from the top and a ray from the bottom of the object.
Use this to explain why the image is inverted.

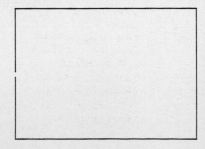

8 Explain in your own words how a bat can find its way in the dark.

9 a) Imagine, in a thunderstorm, lightning strikes 660 metres away from you. Describe and explain what you would observe.
(The speed of sound is 330 metres per second.)
b) A fighter plane flies at a speed of Mach 4. The speed of sound is called Mach 1. How fast is the plane flying?

10 Plan an investigation to see if children have better hearing than adults. How would you make it a fair test?

Index